Praise for *College Ministry in a Post-Christian Culture*

As someone who has ministered to university students in the American South for fifteen years, I cannot thank Steve enough for this book. This is a rare work of theological depth, sociological candor, and methodological wisdom. It is a call to personal renewal for those involved in campus ministry and a field guide for the public reclamation of our campuses for the glory and fame of God. You will not be able to put this down!

—**Matt Adair,** Lead Pastor, Christ Community Church, Athens, GA; Regional Coordinator, The Acts 29 Network

Every once in a while you run across a book that is so "on target" that you just can't put it down. *This is one of those books!* **College Ministry in a Post-Christian Culture** is a must read for anyone wanting to reach today's college students with the good news of Jesus Christ! This book is poised to assist college and campus ministers in making the necessary transitions to a more missional model of ministry, in order to reach an increasingly uninterested target audience, during some of the most formative years of their lives.

—**Dr. Guy Chmieleski,** University Minister, Belmont University

In my experience, college students are some of the best, most effective missionaries in the Church. However, the way God is reaching, developing, and sending out students looks drastically different than it did twenty years ago. This book concisely captures the current movement of God that has the potential to transform existing campus ministries as well as the campuses they engage. I am thrilled to see such a robust theological and practical work for the collegiate context!

—**Todd Engstrom,** Pastor of Missional Communities, The Austin Stone Community Church

College Ministry in a Post-Christian Culture provides the best strategy I have seen for how to reach students (and the institution itself) with the gospel. Steve Lutz clearly explains why college ministry is so desperately needed and offers a missional paradigm to effectively minister to today's students.

—**Derek Melleby,** Author of *Make College Count: A Faithful Guide to Life and Learning*

D1456482

In **College Ministry in a Post-Christian Culture** Steve Lutz provides a much needed resource for understanding and connecting with one of the most strategic ministry people groups in the world—college students. Anyone involved in campus ministry will not want to be without this resource. I really cannot recommend this book more highly.

—**Brad Brisco,** Church Planting Strategist

College Ministry in a Post-Christian Culture is a fresh analysis of the way that church and collegiate ministries view today's college campus. Long gone are the days of campus-wide impact simply through attractional events and meetings. Read this book and get ready to change the way you do ministry!

—**Mark Lydecker,** Student Mobilizer, North American Mission Board

Steve Lutz provides a paradigm shift for college ministry that will determine whether campus ministries actually sustain reciprocal relationships with non-Christian and unchurched students in the future or if the prevailing vision will continue to be simply providing space for Christians to withdraw deeper into "holy huddle" subcultures. Lutz will challenge every campus ministry leader to rethink what it means to love the college campus.

—**Anthony B. Bradley, PhD,** Associate Professor of Theology and Ethics, The King's College (New York City)

Steve Lutz has been making disciples on America's #1 party campus for years. This guy knows what it takes to build an effective outreach to modern college students and shares his experiences in this informative, engaging, and inspiring book.

—**David Murrow,** Author of *Why Men Hate Going to Church*

COLLEGE MINISTRY
IN A POST-CHRISTIAN CULTURE

COLLEGE MINISTRY
IN A POST-CHRISTIAN
CULTURE

Stephen Lutz

the **HOUSE** studio

Copyright 2011 by The House Studio

ISBN 978-0-8341-2765-4

Printed in the United States of America

Cover Design: J.R. Caines
Cover Photo Copyright © 2008 by Cedric Chambaz
Interior Design: Sharon Page

All Scripture quotations not otherwise designated are from the *Holy Bible, New International Version*® (NIV®). Copyright © 1973, 1978, 1984 by International Bible Society. Used by permission of Zondervan. All rights reserved.

www.thehousestudio.com

10 9 8 7 6 5 4 3 2 1

To my wife, Jess
Thanks for going on this mission with me

This book could not have been written without the help of many people. Thank you to the many students at Temple, Penn State, and Philly U who have lived out the stories and fleshed out the theories in this book. Thank you to my colleagues at CCO, New Life, Liberti, and Calvary for providing such great contexts for ministry.

Thank you to my faithful and generous ministry partners for the prayer and financial support that make our ministry possible.

Many friends and colleagues, near and far, have encouraged and sharpened me along the way: Jonathan Weyer, Erica Young Reitz, Geoff Bradford, Dan Nold, Doug Logan, Steve Huber, Dan Wilkinson, Amy Nichols, Tara Atchison, Alan Hirsch, Anthony Bradley, Guy Chmieleski, Kim Rubin, Matt Adair, Mark Lydecker, Chuck Bomar, Todd Engstrom, Denny Henderson, Nick Melazzo, Reggie McNeal, Chris Willard, Brad Brisco, David Murrow, Tony Stiff, Benson Hines, Byron Borger, Derek Melleby, Scott Calgaro, Lizz Heimann, Heather Strong, Steve Baker, Pete Cannizzaro, Aaron Henning, Matt Cohen, Pete Horning, Joe Schafer, Tim Henderson, Dave Bowman, Alex Watlington, Jonny Pons, Buzz Roberts, and Ellen Taricani.

Special thanks to Chris Folmsbee, Kristen Allen, and The House Studio team for your enthusiasm and faith in this project.

Thank you to my in-laws, Gary and Donna Schwenzer, for your assistance in many big and small ways.

Thank you to my parents, Ron and Sue Lutz, for not only modeling faithfulness to the gospel, but faithfully communicating it in all its forms.

Thank you to Samuel, Micah, and Abigail for helping Daddy keep things in perspective through our superhero wrestling matches, monster truck competitions, and trips to the playground. I love being your Daddy.

Finally, thank you to Jess for all the time and energy you gave to make this book possible. More than anyone, you know what this has cost. Thanks for loving me when I was a knuckleheaded college student—and ever since. I am truly blessed.

CONTENTS

Introduction

LOST IN TRANSITION?

*We need to recover the
missional character of
college ministry.*

This is a book for people who love college students. It's a book for campus ministers, church leaders and volunteers, students, and their parents.

This book is about embracing the theology and practice that have fueled the explosive growth of the Church throughout history. It's about applying the power and promise of the gospel of Jesus Christ to life on a college campus.

This book is about ministering to college students during a time of important changes in our culture—changes that present serious challenges, but also wonderful opportunities, to the old way of doing things. It's also about reaching college students during a stage of life that is marked by transition, uncertainty, fear, and seismic shifts in their personal lives.

This book is about seeing college ministry as a unique mission field—what I believe is the most strategic mission field in the world today. It's about changing how we view college students and how we view our roles as ministers, leaders, and servants. It's about doing ministry that is sustainable and fruitful for the long haul.

To reach this generation of college students, we need to make some deep-rooted changes. But to understand why I feel this way, it might help to know how I got here.

How I Ended Up in College Ministry

I never planned on going into college ministry. As an undergrad, I had been actively involved in a fellowship group. God used it to change my life—to call me to vocational ministry, in fact. But like many seminarians, I envisioned myself at a pulpit somewhere, presiding over a large, adoring church. I didn't have anything against college ministry, but as I came to the end of seminary, I envisioned myself doing something...cooler. I thought about jumping on board with a trendy Gen X church (please pardon the term—it was hip when those plans began in 2001) that some friends were planting in Philadelphia. A church plant seemed like a great place for an entrepreneurial guy like me to start his full-time ministry career.

I had a couple problems though: I didn't know how I would fit into the church plant plan, and I wasn't excited about raising financial support.

More like dead set against it. "The last thing I want to do" is what I think I said to my wife, Jess, then pregnant with our first child. I began applying to positions all over the country. Still, I couldn't get the church plant out of my head. In the meantime, my church-planting friends, while out laying groundwork for the church, had met up with some college students who were leaders of Crosswalk, a fellowship group at Temple University. These students were excited about a new church in their backyard. They were feeling somewhat isolated in North Philly because they hadn't found many good places to connect spiritually. Consequently, many of them weren't connecting at all.

I was also starting to hear some unbelievable statistics on college students in that city: with over 300,000 students at more than eighty universities in the metro area, Philadelphia consistently ranks among the top "college towns" in the country.[1] Yet ministry to these students was sorely lacking, to say the least. A school like the University of Pennsylvania, because of its Ivy League cachet, could count on some large parachurch ministries to provide staff and resources. But this wasn't the case for virtually every other campus in Philadelphia, including Temple University, a school of well over 20,000 undergraduates. When I learned there was no full-time evangelical staff presence on the campus, I resolved to visit Crosswalk.

On a cold Thursday night in February, I drove down to Temple's campus. I joined Crosswalk for their large group meeting: I met several more student leaders and settled into my seat. During the worship set, the pieces began falling into place. I saw a small but devoted group of students doing their best to be the body of Christ on campus. I saw their passion for Jesus and their care for one another. I also saw how they struggled on their own. They were "like sheep without a shepherd" (Matthew 9:36). All of it—the statistics, the conversations, the passion and sincerity, the worship, the overwhelming need—left a deep impression on me. It moved me.

Then God *really* got my attention. Immediately following the meeting, I met Jamie, one of the student leaders. I remember very clearly what she said: "We have been praying for years for someone to come lead us and teach us and disciple us. I'm praying that it's you." And with that, I had heard my Macedonian call. How can you say no to an invitation like that? I couldn't. This was no accident. My doubts, while not entirely removed, now paled in comparison to the need of the students I met that night at Crosswalk. I was starting to see the convergence of calling, passion, and need.

So I began raising support and preparing to move my family into the city. Liberti Church, as it came to be known, sent me to lead those students and build a bridge between church and campus. In time, God blessed our church-based campus movement, and we grew to become not only the largest weekly meeting organization on campus, but also the largest Christian gathering of college students in the city. At the time, civic leaders were lamenting the post-college brain drain from the city. But students from our ministry defied the trends and stayed in Philadelphia after graduation. They fulfilled the city-renewing vision of Jeremiah 29: they found jobs, got married, bought homes, and generally blessed the city, all while playing a significant role in the growth and health of our burgeoning church. Many former and current students now hold various leadership roles in that family of churches. Former students and others joined me on staff to shepherd college students, and we branched out to other campuses in our ministry-starved college city.

I wish this story served as the setup to a snazzy model of college ministry that I could unfold throughout the rest of the book as "Five Easy Steps to College Ministry." But there's no formula or recipe. It's not that simple. Ministry that produces lasting fruit never is. The truth is, after several years, I became discontented. Gathering a crowd is not all it's cracked up to be. While we were seeing some conversions every year, I was concerned about the state of many of the students who were filling our seats. We had far too many jaded churched kids—kids who casually attended our large group meeting but were off the radar when it came to finding joy in the gospel, real community, connection to a local church, and a sense of mission on and for our campus. In fact, I came to realize that some of them were substituting our large group meetings for church—the *last* thing I hoped would happen!

In terms of attracting students, we had it all going for us. But we weren't *sending* them. Whatever we were filling up our kids with wasn't overflowing in a way that blessed the campus. We weren't the redemptive presence God wanted us to be. We needed to get on mission. To do that, we needed a truly missional college ministry. This revelation led me to wrestle with the question of what a missional approach to campus ministry would look like: I've been working this out in my own ministry for the past several years. Though much of the church world (especially the church planting world) has been wrestling for many years with what "missional" means, that hasn't been translated into the unique theology and practice of college ministry. This book is intended to address that gap.

Perhaps you're a college minister like me who longs for more. You want more than incremental tweaks; you want to see a shift take place. Perhaps you're a student who longs to see your campus transformed. Perhaps you're a parent whose heart is breaking for your own college student. Perhaps you're a pastor who wants your church to reach the campus in your backyard. Whoever you are, as you read this, I hope you have an experience like my first night at Crosswalk. I want you to hear the statistics. I want you to meet the students. I want you to join in the conversation. But more than anything, I hope this book moves you to action to reach college students.

This book is based on two convictions: 1) college students are the most strategic ministry people group in the world today; and 2) we need to change the ways we reach them in order to help them become more missional. College students are harder to reach than ever, and many leave the church upon reaching college, never to return. Despite some solid efforts and good intentions, church and parachurch organizations are not meeting the urgent need to minister effectively to collegians. We need to recover the missional character of college ministry. The purpose of this book is to translate missional theology to the field of college ministry and to equip college ministry staff, pastors, churches, and student leaders to minister effectively to today's college students.

This book is divided into three parts, using the metaphor of a tree (which I'll explain in chapter one).

Part One: Putting Down Roots

In many ways, college is about the search for identity. This search leads many students to a profound crisis, which is why it is imperative that college ministry be deeply grounded in the gospel. In this section, I define missional theology in practical, accessible terms, and make the case for a missional orientation to college ministry.

Part Two: Growing the Mission

In this section, I flesh out what missional college ministry looks like in practice, describing evangelism, discipleship, and leadership from a missional orientation. I include many stories from my own ministry experience in Philadelphia and at Penn State, especially among skeptics, pagans, Muslims, and other hard-to-reach groups.

Part Three: Fruit That Will Last

Missional college ministry is a proactive movement that is constantly adapting to its ever-changing environment. In this section, I discuss the need for unity and partnership in our ministry efforts. I highlight innovations and some predictions to enable the field of college ministry to not only survive, but thrive in the coming years.

Welcome to *College Ministry in a Post-Christian Culture!* I hope this book leads to transformation in you, your ministry, and your campus.

Part One

PUTTING DOWN ROOTS

THE GOSPEL, COMMUNITY, AND THE MISSIO DEI

Chapter 1
FROM TUMBLEWEED TO TREE

What are the roots that clutch, what branches grow
Out of this stony rubbish? Son of man,
You cannot say, or guess, for you know only
A heap of broken images, where the sun beats,
And the dead tree gives no shelter, the cricket no relief,
And the dry stone no sound of water . . .
And I will show you something different from either
Your shadow at morning striding behind you
Or your shadow at evening rising to meet you;
I will show you fear in a handful of dust.
—T. S. Eliot, *The Waste Land*

Tumbleweeds are stubborn things. As I looked out the window, about twenty of them reclined against the fence, looking back at me smugly. My wife and I were visiting our friends Brent and Jodi in the desert of Arizona. Being from Pennsylvania, the only tumbleweeds I was familiar with were the animated Wile E. Coyote types or the single tumbleweed rolling down the deserted street before the obligatory gunfight in an old Western movie. So I was surprised to learn from Jodi that tumbleweeds are in fact numerous and quite a nuisance. With little to no root system, they are easily picked up and tossed around by the wind. As I watched them, they blew across their desert setting until they all met up for a prearranged party at my friends' fence.

The day before, in an effort to be helpful to them, I had gathered up all the tumbleweeds I could find and carted them off to a sort of dumping ground a few hundred feet from their home. Yet there they were again, the very next day, all stacked up against the fence. Simply shuffling the tumbleweeds hadn't produced any lasting improvements to the landscape. My brilliant plan had failed and had made me feel foolish.

Ministry in the Wasteland

The world is changing rapidly: if you're a campus minister, a student leader, a pastor or church leader, a parent, or just someone who cares about college students, you know that the collegiate mission field is no exception. In fact, it's leading the way in change, and many of us in ministry are struggling to catch up. We're busy chasing and rearranging those tumbleweeds, but it's hard to feel like we're getting anywhere.

What makes the work of college ministry feel a bit like we're collecting tumbleweeds? The first challenge is our landscape. We live and serve in a post-Christian wasteland, a desert landscape bereft of the living water of Christ. As a result, the context of our ministry feels increasingly resistant to our efforts. The shift from colleges as bastions of pastoral training to secular hotbeds is not a new phenomenon, but the shift we're talking about is more recent, a shift that's been so fast and far-reaching that many college ministers are still reeling, still trying to make sense of it all.

We are experiencing a transition from what has been called "Christendom" to a largely post-Christian society. The shift to a post-Christian society has been well under way in the rest of the Western world for several decades, but it has been felt in the U.S. only more recently. Christendom existed wherever the dominant culture reflected Christian belief and behavior, and it had a long heyday. For at least one thousand years, the Church in the West could assume that people would be "Christianized," though not necessarily converted, by society.

In that context, ministries could take a lot for granted. People generally believed in the Christian, triune God, at least intellectually. They believed in sin. When we talked about concepts like faith, hope, and love, they generally knew what we meant. When we talked about how people "should" live, the Church could fall back on a cultural consensus that was fairly compatible with its message. Everyone in town went to church: those who didn't were ostracized. Other institutions in society reinforced Christian morality: stores were closed on Sunday, and towns enforced blue laws.

It wasn't long ago that this world existed. In some pockets of the country, it still does. I'm not arguing for a return to this world. Not only is that not going to happen, but Christendom wasn't all good. The prevailing complaints against the Church, the rise of the New Atheism movement, and the spread of multitudinous, personally-determined spiritualities are signposts to the reaction against, and rejection of, Christendom. There's an element of prophetic rebuke to these developments that we need to heed. And as you'll see in this book, I believe our new context is filled with exciting opportunities, but we can rise up to meet them only if we know what they are.

While the Christendom context certainly had its challenges, it also had its opportunities. Whole aspects of society performed what amounted to a massive "sowing" effort, educating people on Christian thought and ethics so the Church could focus on reaping through the personal, experiential aspects of faith. The Church's role was to pick the low-hanging, "Christianized" fruit. A traveling evangelist or a student with a booklet could draw on the cultural consensus and lay out a simple gospel message, and scores of people would enter into relationship with Jesus. In many places today, ministry continues under the assumption that large groups of Christianized people will continue to walk through their doors, needing only an invitation to "receive Christ." Many churches and ministries still operate as if their neighbors are familiar with the Bible and are in basic agreement with a Christian worldview and ethic. But this is increasingly, and emphatically, not the case.

On many of our campuses today, all this seems like the quaint relic of a long gone, even alien, era. We now live in a post-Christian mission field. In many parts of the country, we could go even further and say the people there are *pre*-Christian. Occasionally, I encounter people who say, "This country has been reached! Shouldn't our efforts be focused elsewhere?" If that's you, I invite you to spend a weekend on a college campus. Make sure you get out of the Christian bubble, and see if you feel the same way on Sunday afternoon. For those of us who live in the U.S., missiologists are now saying we live in the fifth largest mission field in the world.[1] So, congratulations! We are, by default, missionaries.

On Penn State University's campus, where I currently minister, there are approximately 44,000 students. Our best estimates are that approximately 1,200 to 1,500 of those students are regularly involved in Christian fellowship through a parachurch group or local church. That's about 2.5 percent of the student body, *or less than the percentage of professing Christians in Communist China,* where people can face criminal charges for operating outside of the state-sanctioned church. No heavy-handed governmental restrictions are necessary here. This isn't just Penn State, by the way—this is true of campuses all over North America.

Praying at Temple

I served for nearly five years as a pastor in Philadelphia, where I worked extensively with students from Temple University. Temple was founded by an influential turn of the (twentieth) century pastor named Russell Conwell. Temple began as a school for training Baptist pastors.

The little neighborhood in North Philly where Temple now sits was renowned for its kingdom work. But during the twentieth century, things changed. Temple officially disaffiliated itself from the Baptist Church (and in the process, sent its divinity school up to Massachusetts to help form Gordon-Conwell Theological Seminary). The old congregation relocated to the suburbs, and the old Baptist Temple church building, from which the school got its name, until recently lay rotting on North Broad Street.

In the past, seeing students gathered together to pray on Temple's campus was not only a common event; it was expected. But when Crosswalk, the group I led, set up a prayer tent at the center of campus, someone started a Facebook group called F#$@ Crosswalk. I don't tell this story because our experience was particularly unique. It wasn't. You can probably tell similar stories from your college ministry experiences. But these stories are significant because they remind us that ministry on college campuses has changed.

And the cultural consensus hasn't just broken down. I would argue that it has decidedly shifted to some very different values. For all the talk of diversity, the norm on many of our campuses is startlingly uniform: relativistic personal morality, shape-shifting sexuality, a crusading "save the world" idealism by day and a debaucherous "party as if the world is ending" nihilism by night. The rootlessness of modern life has produced what sociologists are saying is a new, distinct life stage, called "emerging adulthood." Many people between eighteen and thirty view themselves as neither children nor fully responsible and engaged adults. They're staying in school longer, delaying marriage longer, trying more careers on for size, and living longer on Mom and Dad's financial support.

Noted sociologist Christian Smith has reviewed several books on emerging adulthood, including *Generation Me* by Jean Twenge, which describes the paradox of this generation's identity: free, confident, tolerant, open-minded, and self-asserting, but also cynical, depressed, lonely, and anxious. How did this happen? Smith observes that

> multiple mainstream institutions in our culture have taught them
> their entire lives "to put their own needs first and to focus on feeling

good about themselves," encouraging them to believe that they can be whatever they want to be, that self-esteem is everything, conformity to rules is ridiculous, easy sexual fulfillment is waiting to be had, and life is all about consumption and gratification . . . Having actually believed such confident messages, young adults then find it hard to cope when real life often turns out differently. Stagnant careers, failed romances, personal insecurities, financial difficulties, and other disappointments and problems often lead to sarcasm, depression, apprehension, loneliness, and self-defeating gambits to force life to turn out the way it was promised to have worked.[2]

Fear in a Handful of Dust

These shifts have produced a wasteland landscape that is not without its bitter consequences for today's students. Billy Graham once asked former Harvard president Derek Bok, "What is the biggest problem among today's students?" Bok answered, "Emptiness."[3] My time with students has led me to agree with Bok. Among college students, certainties and absolutes are dismissed as naive at best. The search itself is seen as the highest attainable goal, so students are discouraged from putting down their roots to any significant depth. Consequently, they are like tumbleweeds—without roots and "blown and tossed by the wind" (James 1:6). They are "harassed and helpless, like sheep without a shepherd" (Matthew 9:36). Look for a moment past all the energy, idealism, and partying on today's college campuses, and "I will show you fear in a handful of dust."[4]

But please don't misunderstand me when I describe college campuses as a wasteland. I love the vitality, creativity, and opportunity of the modern university. I think our campuses are among the most exciting places to be in the world today. They are like our greatest cities in that respect. And like our great cities, they simultaneously display both the best and the worst of humanity.

So what should we do? How can we live as Christians in the wasteland? How can we lead strong ministries to today's students in the wasteland? Large sectors of the Church have expended a great deal of energy in reacting to and fighting against cultural forces, such as rejecting pluralism, insisting on the maintenance of Christianity's privileged place in the public square, and generally trying to turn back the clock to Christendom. But this is not the answer; this misguided project has failed. But neither is the answer to just give in and accept the bargain offered by relativism—"we'll leave you alone if you leave us alone"—and retreat to the exceedingly private, individualistic Christian faith bubble that does little to engage the world.

Our context and culture have shifted, and college ministry needs to shift as well. It's not a shift to something new, but something old. We need to recover the *missio Dei*, the mission of God, God's mission to redeem, renew, and restore a broken world. We didn't come up with this idea— God did. Since Genesis 3, God has never ceased in his redemptive work. But we easily forget about the missio Dei. Missional college ministry worthy of the name seeks to join God in God's mission to reach our college contexts. Missional college ministry looks to the Bible, God's unfolding story of redemption, for answers. The Bible is our foundation.

Before we can talk missional strategies—which this book will do—we need to gain a firm footing. Otherwise, we're just one more breeze blowing across the wasteland. While the situation on campus may feel new to us, it's not new to humanity or to God. Jeremiah 17:5-6 describes the "tumbleweed" phenomenon quite well:

> This is what the LORD says: "Cursed is the one who trusts in man, who depends on flesh for his strength and whose heart turns away from the LORD. He will be like a bush in the wastelands; he will not see prosperity when it comes. He will dwell in the parched places of the desert, in a salt land where no one lives."

What our students are experiencing isn't just a twenty-first century, Western phenomenon. Nor is it best explained by life stage or generational theories. And it's certainly not just affecting our colleges.

Ultimately, it's a manifestation of life apart from God. Students attend college for all kinds of reasons, but when pressed, their reasons tend to boil down to having fun and making money. Sex and pleasure, power, and wealth—this is what students look to for life and meaning. All the education and extracurriculars that higher education has to offer amount to a dependence on "flesh for strength," which disappoints our students, leads to the "cursed life," and leaves them parched, "like a bush in the wastelands." Does this language sound strong? If so, consider why this generation is more medicated and depressed than ever,[5] more socially connected, yet simultaneously starved for genuine relationship. Ask yourself why students are afraid to stand in one place for more than a moment.

Tumbleweed students are addicted to change. They change their majors, their schools, their cities, and will change their careers several times. They change their friends, their partners, their sexualities. They change their hair, their clothes, their bodies, their entire looks. They change their personalities, their causes, their beliefs. At the end of all that change, what do they have to show for it? They are still the same old tumbleweeds.

But it's not just students who are addicted to change. Ministries—and their ministers—are just as guilty. We change our worship style from contemporary to traditional to rock to spoken word to neo-traditional and back to contemporary. We change our teaching style from topical to exegetical to conversational and back again. We change our large group meetings from sing and speaks to worship concerts to discipleship groups to game nights to *no* large groups and back again. We change our leadership groups, our discipleship processes, our vision and mission documents, our strategic plans. If all that fails, we change our campus, our coworkers, the organization we work for, or we leave ministry entirely.

And yet, very little seems to be actually changing. The more we've changed things, the more we feel unmoored, parched, and fruitless. What do we do when we've changed everything, but nothing's really changed?

Why Doesn't Change Work?

Why don't these conspicuous change strategies work? Why do they always fail to deliver the hope that we and our students long for? Because these kinds of changes don't go down to where the problem is, to the roots. They can't in a rootless system. Fortunately, the gospel transforms us from inside out, down to the roots, at the heart level. We see this as Jeremiah continues in chapter seventeen, verses seven and eight:

> "But blessed is the man who trusts in the LORD, whose confidence is in him. He will be like a tree planted by the water that sends out its roots by the stream. It does not fear when heat comes; its leaves are always green. It has no worries in a year of drought and never fails to bear fruit."

The gospel is best understood when we connect our story to God's story. Using Jeremiah's picture of a tree, we can express it like this: God created us to please him, to enjoy him, and to give him glory. We are meant to be full of his life (John 10:10) and to display his glorious creativity.

But sin entered the world, and we are both its victims and perpetrators. Sin has alienated us from God, ourselves, other people, and the rest of God's creation. We frequently minimize sin, but the truth is this: left to ourselves, we are the bush in the wastelands. We are the dead, rolling tumbleweed. We cannot bring ourselves to life, no matter how many times we change our circumstances. We are more lost, more withered, more fruitless, and more dead than we would ever want to admit. We are justly deserving of God's punishment for our sins. None of us, no matter how intelligent, educated, or successful we are, can save ourselves.

Luckily for us, that's not the end of the story because God intervenes through Jesus Christ—Jesus, who the Bible says became the curse of God for us by hanging on *a tree*. "For it is written: 'Cursed is everyone who is hung on a tree'" (Galatians 3:13). As Christian counselor and author David Powlison has noted, through the lens of Christ we see three trees in Jeremiah 17.[6] It is through the tree of the cross that we are brought from dead bush to thriving tree. Jesus restores our relationship to God by taking the curse of our sins on himself and giving us his perfect life. He makes it possible to see ourselves rightly. He reconciles us to one another, making genuine community possible. Through his resurrection, we are members of his new creation. We join him in redeeming and renewing his creation, restoring it and cultivating it to God's original intent.

Through him we have access to the "full" life he promised in John 10:10. It is the work of the Christian life to believe in Jesus and his gospel (John 6:36). Abandoning our confidence in ourselves, we take hold of the gospel—not merely as the starting point, but as the foundation of *all* that we are and do. Abandoning our faith in change itself, we put our roots down *deep* in God. I love Jeremiah's imagery of the tree planted by the water. No matter how hot the environment gets, the tree will not only survive, but *thrive*, because its roots go all the way down to the living water. In Christ, we can be strong, confident, green, and fruitful trees. This is good news for those of us who live in the heat of college ministry environments.

What missional college ministers, pastors, students, and parents have to offer to today's students is the promise of being rooted in God himself. The danger for Christian ministries is that we provide only one more costume for students to try on during their college years. When this is the case, Christian faith becomes one more phase, something they easily put on and take off. But without our own proper foundation, we're just tumbleweeds gathering tumbleweeds, surprised to see them blown and tossed around the next day. We need to stop merely entertaining. We need to stop doing lame impressions of "fun college life." (You heard me, root beer kegger.) We need to stop competing in the college attention game and start sending the message that we're playing for higher stakes. We need to call them to put their roots down into something solid.

We must also be careful to go all the way down to the fullness of the gospel, not false or partial versions. The gospel is about personal salvation, but it's also about God's redemptive plan for the renewal of *all things*. Reducing it to an individualistic, formulaic exchange leaves people with a been-there-done-that mentality and robs them of a view of the glorious scope of redemption—and it also robs God of his glory. Similarly, reducing the gospel to concern about the poor or the environment while minimizing personal aspects robs God and harms people. We must always fight against our tendency to reduce the gospel to less than it is. It is the starting point of the Christian life, but we never move beyond it. We need to send the message that to be rooted in the gospel isn't the end, but only the beginning.

Just in case we're tempted to go back and say "I've already heard this" or "I already know this," or to trust ourselves and our own devices, Jeremiah offers a preemptive rebuke in chapter seventeen, verse nine: "The heart is deceitful above all things and beyond cure. Who can understand it?" We fool ourselves. We're easily deluded by our thirst. We might even stand in the middle of the desert and call it a vacation at the beach. "Look—I've got sand, my umbrella, my towel, and some sunscreen! This is a blast!" Yes, but we have no *water*! We won't find life there. We're in the wasteland!

Make Like a Tree

The tree metaphor is a powerful one in Scripture. The Psalms begin with this word picture, which serves as a frame for the entire book of worship. Isaiah makes extensive use of the tree, talking about the "shoot," the "branch," and "oaks of righteousness." And the tree serves as a good picture of our relationship to Christ: being grounded in the gospel, growing in community, and giving in mission. Or in other words, our roots, our trunk, and our fruit.

Before we did anything, before we *were* anything, God loved us first. He's the initiator. He's the one who makes us grow. We may start with the smallest seed, and by God's grace, see it grow into a mighty tree. The truth of the gospel is the power of God (Romans 1:16) for life, for transformation, for all we need (2 Peter 1:3). Our gospel roots determine what kind of trees we will be. They determine our identity as a child of God, as a new creation, a new person.

Before a tree ever bears fruit, it must first tap into life-giving sources. God's free and gracious love for us precedes our responses of worship and good works (Ephesians 2:8-10). I'm no arborist, but I know that the bigger a tree is, the more extensive its root system will be. In fact, I'm told that a tree's root system is just as big as its branch system. In the same way, we also need to be deeply rooted to our own source of life. If we're to be healthy, we should be growing: bigger, stronger, and healthier. The more we're rooted in good soil and tapped into life-giving water, the more we can grow, whether or not we're surrounded by a wasteland. The mature, healthy tree will bear fruit, and so should we—the kind of "fruit that will last," according to Jesus' words in John 15:16.

Notice three key implications of our metaphor. The first is that life and growth move from the bottom up, through the roots, trunk, and fruit. Through the process of transpiration, life-giving nutrients flow from roots to fruit. The tree imagery is a reminder that reaching a new stage does not mean leaving the previous one. We never move on from our roots—we only grow deeper. Just as no tree bears fruit unless it has a healthy root system, so no believer can bear fruit (at least over the long term) unless he or she is grounded and growing in the transforming power of the gospel.

The second is that our tree is "organic." Many of us in ministry circles love this term, and I know my more scientifically-oriented readers are grimacing right now because I don't mean "carbon based." For our purposes "organic" means *natural*, as opposed to industrial or mechanistic. The reason the Bible uses agricultural images so often is not only because they are so accessible (to their original audience, especially), but because they inherently communicate the importance of life, health, growth, and of course, reproduction.

The third implication is this: just as bearing fruit is not an optional add-on for a fruit tree, but the very thing it was created to do, so must mission not be considered an optional add-on to our ministry, but integral to anything and everything we do. It's not extra!

Two Important Questions

I have two very important questions for you, questions you should answer before you go any further in this book. The first is this: *Does the grounded, growing, fruitful tree describe you?* Can you say that you are firmly rooted in the gospel, not tossed around every few days or weeks? Is your foundation resting on ministry performance or the approval of others? Many of us aspire to have wide, expansive branches of ministry, but do you have an even greater ambition for your root system to go deeper into the gospel?

My wife grew up in a neighborhood that featured some newfangled genetically engineered trees. They were beautiful and full. They were top-heavy with branches and leaves, but it turned out that the genetic modifications had left them with puny root systems. As you might expect, they didn't last long. In a relatively short time, wind and storms had felled nearly every single one. Everyone in the neighborhood eventually had to cut them down and plant new ones. Top-heavy trees don't last very long—only until the next big storm. And being top-heavy with shallow roots is a tragedy when it comes to people and ministries. Be honest with yourself—because if the healthy tree doesn't describe you, it won't do you much good to dive into mission. One tumbleweed can't do much for other tumbleweeds. The best thing you can do for your ministry is to start with yourself and get grounded in the gospel.

My next question is like the first: *Does the grounded, growing, fruitful tree describe your ministry?* The tree doesn't just work on an individual level, but on a corporate level as well. Many times we come up with the wrong answers because we ask the wrong questions. Pastor Jonathan Dodson says that we need to raise the problem of mission and answer it with the gospel, in the context of community.[7] Change any of those around, and you lose them. If your ministry isn't on mission, it *doesn't* mean that you just need to try harder to get on mission. It means that you're not as grounded or growing as you think you are.

Let me show you how the right answers to the wrong questions can lead us astray. Let's take one of the pathologies plaguing virtually every campus ministry I know: the nominal involvement of students who visit a different ministry every night of the week or don't feel the need for any ministry at all. As college ministers, we're familiar with the chorus of students who say, "I don't need other people to be spiritual." This opinion is only reinforced by their ability to listen to their favorite preacher online, read their favorite blogs, and pop in and out of groups when they feel like it. This type of hyper-individualistic Christian faith is *totally* foreign to biblical Christianity.

But we make a critical mistake when we say, "These students aren't connecting! Our community isn't accepting/welcoming/edifying enough! We need to work on our community!" So we organize lengthy vision-casting sessions with our leaders. We read some books on community (hopefully this one), maybe go to a conference or two. We do a teaching series on community in our large group setting (preferably from one of Paul's epistles). We schedule some extra community-building events. Whether we say it or not, we communicate that community is our problem, and community is our goal. And then we wonder, "Why is our group so inward-facing, so non-missional?" Easy! Because that's what we've taught them to be! Community isn't the answer, but neither is mission—the gospel is. We need each of these elements, but we need them in their proper place and in proper relationship to each other.

Let me offer another example—the group known for its strong biblical, doctrinal, and teaching emphases. Their students know the Scriptures inside and out. They memorize tons of verses. Open up to a random page of the Bible, and they could lead an informative study. They can wax eloquent on fine points of theology. We see groups that know their Bible or their doctrine, but they don't know any non-Christians. They're adept at arguing with other Christians but ill-equipped to have a meaningful conversation with someone who doesn't know or follow Christ.

It breaks God's heart when his story of redemption just becomes fodder for discussion among the already converted. And what do you think happens to community in groups like this? Like an old preacher once told me, "If you ain't fishin', you're fightin'." Theology apart from mission leads us to turn on each other. It seems this is part of what happened in the Galatian church. Out of distaste for the mission to the Gentiles, the Judaizers shut it down and majored on the minors (like circumcision). In doing so, they lost sight of the gospel, to the extent that Paul said, "If you keep on biting and devouring each other, watch out or you will be destroyed by each other" (Galatians 5:15). Ouch! Make no mistake; we're capable of the same thing.

Another example: the outreach-focused, evangelistic, seeker-sensitive group. They're on mission, right? Well, they may have raised the problem of mission, but often they do not answer that with a robust gospel foundation. The problem of mission is answered with mission, and what should be a rich, deep, challenging, and accountable community becomes a soul-sucking, burnout-inducing, mile-wide and inch-deep outreach association. Even more disturbing, the gospel can be redefined to become more amenable to the mission, and many partial and even false variations of the gospel ensue.

Growing Oaks of Righteousness

As we close this chapter, imagine with me what kind of tree you aspire your ministry to be like. Some trees are impressive for their sheer size, like redwoods or giant sequoias. The biggest one, General Sherman in Sequoia National Park, stands at over 275 feet tall. Each year, it adds enough wood to its own mass to make a regular sixty-foot tall tree. Other trees are known for their age and resiliency. The oldest known living tree in the world is in California, a bristlecone pine named Methuselah, after the biblical figure who lived to be 969 years old. The Methuselah tree is not that impressive—until you learn that it is *4,838 years old*. It is not only the oldest tree, but also the oldest living non-clonal organism in the world.

Other trees are known for their reproductive ability. The Trembling Giant in Utah is technically a single quaking aspen tree but with *thousands* of "stems" that spring up looking like separate trees. All the stems are part of a single living organism with an enormous underground root system. Talk about being well grounded! My favorite tree though may be the baobab tree. Baobabs can grow to almost one hundred feet tall and thirty-five feet wide. They're known for their ability to store water: their thick, swollen trunks can store as much as 30,000 gallons of water to survive the driest desert conditions.[8]

All these are Jeremiah 17 kinds of trees! They serve as perfect pictures of the kind of ministries we're seeking to build—strong, resilient, wildly reproductive, and resourceful. Trees that provide grounding and a solid foundation in an uncertain time of life. Trees that provide strength and protection amid the storm. Trees that provide shade, comfort, and fruit. Trees that make their environment more beautiful. Trees that are, in a word, *redemptive*. Isaiah captures this concept well:

> They will be called oaks of righteousness, a planting of the LORD for the display of his splendor. They will rebuild the ancient ruins and restore the places long devastated; they will renew the ruined cities that have been devastated for generations. (Isaiah 61:3*b*-4)

Now that's the kind of mission worth growing!

Chapter 2

WHAT IS MISSIONAL?

A looming crisis for all American evangelical churches is that they cannot thrive outside of the shrinking enclaves of conservative and traditional people and culture.[1]

—Tim Keller

A while back, I spoke with the leaders of a large college fellowship group with whom I have a relationship. They are devoted to reaching their campus and had recently rolled out an extensive plan that would equip their students to reach their non-Christian friends, roommates, and classmates. Everyone seemed enthusiastic and on board until the president of the group voiced his concern: "It's great to reach out to our non-Christian friends; *the only problem is that I don't have any.*"

The staff was rightly appalled and grieved. Somehow, the ministry they had built had cut off their most committed leaders from the very campus they were seeking to reach! The more responsibility the student leaders took on, the more they were helping drive the organizational engine, but the less they were on mission. The staff resolved to make sweeping changes. No one wants to see the tragic irony of Christians who are too busy "doing ministry" to reach out to non-Christians. I'm happy to say this group is making some big changes and seeing good fruit from those changes.

Sadly, this group isn't alone. The evangelical Church in America is not thriving outside of our usual enclaves. While we can likely think of some thriving churches, on the whole, the Church in North America is shrinking. Approximately 3,700 churches close their doors for good every year, while 4,000 are planted. This sounds good until you realize that a net gain of 300 is only 10 percent of what's needed to keep pace with population growth. One study estimated that 100,000 churches in North America will close in the next seven years (out of the 350,000 in existence)![2]

And our college ministries are suffering as well. How can we break out and reach the rapidly growing sectors of postmodern, post-Christian people? What are effective missional models for doing this? What *is* missional college ministry, anyway, and how does it differ from traditional college ministry? While the evangelical church has been wrestling with the theological and practical implications of being missional for over a decade, this reflection is notably deficient in the college ministry world—one of the fields in which it is *most* needed.

I know many college ministers who share my nagging sense that something is wrong. Being humbled by two realizations, we agree that old approaches to ministry are no longer sufficient. First, we are ministering to the largest college-going generation of all time (nearly sixteen million undergraduates in 2009, according to the U.S. Census Bureau). The class of 2010 was the largest graduating class ever, and enrollment is expected to remain high through 2015, economy permitting.[3] So while campus ministries' raw numbers may be up, our per capita numbers, and often our staff-to-student ratios, are way down.

Second, most college ministries are not breaking much new ground. The Ivy Jungle Network's State of Campus Ministry survey in 2008 found that the majority of campus ministries see only *one to five* conversions each year.[4] Many of the groups are growing by becoming more efficient at attracting students from the increasingly smaller pockets of Christendom.

Why the lack of fruitfulness in campus ministry? Simple. *Many campus ministry models are not inherently missional.* This might strike you as counterintuitive if not offensive. Let me be clear: I am *not* saying that people engaged in campus ministry don't care about reaching non-Christians. I'm assuming the reason many of us are in college ministry is evangelism. I believe many of us have missional aspects in our ministries. But much of campus ministry does not have mission built into its DNA.

What do I mean? Traditional ministry treats mission or outreach as something we *do* while "missional" is something we *are*: mission shifts from an activity to our identity. We are the people of God, on God's mission. As Paul says in 2 Corinthians, it is Christ's love that compels us to make the gospel message known, by transforming us from self-absorbed creatures into ambassadors of the gospel of Christ:

> For Christ's love compels us, because we are convinced that one died for all, and therefore all died. And he died for all, that those who live should no longer live for themselves but for him who died for them and was raised again. (5:14-15)

As God's gospel-transformed and sent people, we orient everything we do to God's mission, which is to reconcile and restore God's fallen creation to himself through his son Jesus Christ. This is what we mean by "missional." This reclaiming of our identity changes *everything*. Nothing is the same; our entire Christian life takes on a new tone and quality—a new ethos. The missional ethos is well expressed by Paul in I Corinthians: "I have become all things to all men so that by all possible means I might save some. I do all this for the sake of the gospel, that I may share in its blessings" (9:22*b*-23).

So why do we settle for "doing mission" *some* of the time? Why do we settle for *some* "outreach" events every semester, as if we need a special reason to invite people? Why do we think a big name speaker or a special concert or event is even close to sufficient? Mission is not something for *some* of us. It is not something we do *some* of the time. Mission is for all Christians all the time.

Being missional goes beyond "doing missions." We need to go further than telling ourselves and our students, "Hey, we're all missionaries now." That sentiment, while laudable in its intent, can still send the message that being a missionary is some kind of special function for a season. Living on mission goes all the way down to the core of our being. It is how we express our identity as citizens of the kingdom of God. Every Christian is called and sent to the world just as Jesus was sent into the world: "As the Father has sent me, so I am sending you" (John 20:21). Missional people perceive themselves as sent people; their underlying attitude toward themselves and their world shifts as a result.

Unfortunately, we easily lose the comprehensive missional ethos. We think, "Well, we're on campus—isn't that being sent?" Showing up is a big part of being missional, but it's not the only part. Many of our ministries fall short of our missional calling because we assume proximity is the same thing as missional purpose. We do all sorts of good things but without a missional orientation.

A ministry may excel at mobilizing students for personal evangelism every week, but its various large and small group meetings feel utterly closed to non-Christians. Another ministry may teach students a great deal about the Bible or scripture memory, but that Bible knowledge never seems to touch down in the reality of their classwork, relationships, and decisions. A ministry may excel at community service, but with little thought as to how they are spreading the good news of the kingdom. A ministry might emphasize equipping their students with a Christian world-view, but these same students don't share their knowledge with others. All of these are good things, but it's possible to do all sorts of good things without a missional orientation.

We serve in Higher Ed, an arena generally further down the road to post-Christendom than the rest of society. Yet many campus ministries have operated in denial because they can still draw a crowd among students who are already churched and converted or inclined to be traditional and conservative. But those "markets" are shrinking. One reason many of us in campus ministry are despairing is because we sense that we are merely carving up our shrinking slice of the "pie" instead of growing our share. Our evangelism falls on dear ears, and the unchurched seem further than ever from Christ.

Ministries may proliferate on our campus, but they end up competing for the same pool of previously Christianized students. Instead of being lights to the world around them, many campus ministries appear to be more like holy huddles. Michael Green has described this ghetto tendency in the church, noting that Christians act like "a community of immigrants in a foreign country, clinging together for warmth and understanding, and surrounded by a society that does not understand or seem to care."[5] We have to resist the urge to ghettoize, to reach only the previously reached. For example, where I serve in Pennsylvania, we have many students who come from our own little Bible Belt, the "buckle" of which is centered on the highly religious, highly Christendom area around Lancaster. Traditional college ministry models generally do well among groups like this but often prove unadaptable to less churched students.

While doing better among the large pools of more traditional students at large, suburban or rural schools, many college ministries seem to have a particularly difficult time staffing those places that are farthest down the road to a post-Christian world. The Ivy Jungle Network found that only 25 percent of the ministries they surveyed were located in the Northeast and West Coast—"the most populous areas of the country have the least involvement."[6] If churched Bible Belt kids are the only students we're reaching, we are not being faithful to the missional call.

Why We Need Missional College Ministry

A missional orientation to campus ministry recognizes that, for at least three reasons, reaching students *now* is imperative to the health and future of the Church and the kingdom of God in North America and around the world:

The need is urgent: The Barna Group found that the vast majority (77 percent) of professions of faith come before or during the college years. Yet according to Thom Rainer, only 15 percent of the current college-going generation identify themselves as Christians. Close to 70 million people in this generation are not Christians;[7] they make up the largest mission field we've ever seen in North America. There are many schools out there with very little ministry and shepherding going on. Crowds of students are coming through every day, and no one is there to reach them. College ministry has the unique problem of being vastly under-reached.

The challenge is huge: The study that formed the basis for *UnChristian* by David Kinnaman and Gabe Lyons found that of non-Christian people ages sixteen to twenty-nine, only 16 percent have a favorable view of Christianity, and only 3 percent have a favorable view of evangelicals.[8] Nearly half of non-Christians agree with the statement, "Christians get on my nerves," and two-thirds agree that "the Church is full of hypocrites."[9] Spend some time on your local campus—preferably after midnight on a Saturday night—and you will see how great our challenge is. But these problems are opportunities to explore better ways of doing things, to get rid of the same old methods. It's an opportunity to shed outdated—and unbiblical—perceptions of Christianity, and take on the skin of something more authentically Christlike.

These people groups are strategic: It may be an understatement to say that "perhaps the most important mission field in contemporary America is the college campus."[10] Higher Ed students make up nearly 7 percent of our national population (20.5 million undergraduate and graduate students according to 2006 census data). But because these people grow to be leaders in every sphere, the impact they have on the world far exceeds their numbers. I'll go ahead and make what may be a controversial statement: *College ministry is the most strategic mission field in the world today.*

It is the most strategic because of *who* comprises this people group—the top 1 percent of the world's population privileged enough to go to college, the future leaders of the world. The college campus is also significant from a global missions perspective, bringing students from nearly every nation of the world to our doorstep for a few crucial years. Recently, I was invited by our Muslim Student Association to be the Christian representative on an interfaith panel, along with a rabbi and an imam. (Sounds like the start of a joke, right?) I shared the gospel with a room full of Muslims, most of them from the Middle East, and many from countries that do not tolerate much, if any, Christian expression. For thirty uninterrupted minutes, I got to share the gospel with more Muslims than a missionary in many Muslim countries can reach in a year. I do not say this to denigrate the work of missionaries in Muslim countries but to highlight the incredible opportunities in our backyard.

College students are also strategic because of *when* they are. We're all aware of how profoundly formative this stage of life can be. The college years powerfully shape the lives of men and women, setting the trajectory of their entire lives. It is during this time that they make essential decisions about their identity, beliefs, and ethics—what they will study and do, whom they will befriend, hook up with, perhaps date and marry. Underlying all of these questions is the foundational question of whether God will have any part in helping students make these decisions. It is crucial that the Church be present in the lives of students—both Christian and non-Christian—during this key stage of life. College offers a window of opportunity before the rest of their life crowds in.

Finally, college students are strategic because of *where* they are. The modern campus is an incredibly strategic location—a place devoted to the exchange of ideas and figuring out what to believe. In New Testament times, Paul went to the synagogue, the marketplace, and Mars Hill (*Areopagus*) to proclaim the gospel. Today, I'm sure he would make college campuses among his first priority because like no other institution in the world, they combine all three. I know no other place in our society where worship, business, and the exchange of ideas are combined so powerfully, freely, *and* personally. We just don't get these opportunities anywhere else!

More Than a Fad

I must emphasize that being missional is not just the latest ministry fad. Being missional is not merely a new technique or warmed-over seeker-sensitivity for bored churched kids. It is the fruit of thoughtful biblical and theological reflection upon how the Church can be faithful and proactive in a time of change.

Admittedly, and regrettably, for some people "missional" has taken on fad-like qualities and become the latest hip adjective to throw in when discussing our ministries. When we hear the word missional, we should have a healthy skepticism as to how people are using it. But despite abuses of the term, it's a good one, and we should closely examine our ministries to see if they are truly missional. The best question we can ask again and again is, How does this help us join God in his mission to redeem and renew the world?

Chapter 3
TEN SHIFTS TO MISSIONAL COLLEGE MINISTRY

We must continually ask,
What does it look like to
communicate and incarnate
the gospel in this particular place,
at this particular time, to this
particular people?

In college ministry, it's no longer enough to attract a crowd. We have to mobilize our students for mission. The current practices of college ministry are not only less than the biblical ideal; they can be startlingly ineffective. We need a missional shift. As people on mission, we willingly and intentionally change our methods. We become beings who are different from—maybe even undesirable to—our natural selves in order to introduce people to Jesus Christ for the sake of the gospel. With this thought in mind, let's take a look at ten shifts to missional college ministry that you can start making *right now*.

Shift #1: From Religion and Relationship to Gospel

One place we need to shift is in how we define and explain what Christianity is about. It's become common for well-meaning Christians to say, "Being a Christian is not about religion. It's about a relationship." But in our post-Christendom era, this line is both tired and discounted by the unchurched and dechurched. Secularists rightfully point out much that is still "religious" about the Christian faith. (If they're really savvy, they'll reference verses like 1 Timothy 5:4 and James 1:26-27.) Neither do they find talk of relationship very persuasive, especially because non-Christian "spiritual" people already have a crowded buffet of spiritual relationships from which to choose.

Both "religion" and "relationship" capture helpful aspects of what Christianity is, but neither word is strong enough to fully encapsulate what Christianity is about. Only "gospel" can do that. When the New Testament authors (especially Jesus) want to sum up what they're about, they invariably come back to *euangelion*, which is Greek for "gospel" or "good news." The gospel is the first thing out of Jesus' mouth as he begins his ministry (Mark 1:15). He equates the gospel with himself in Mark 8:35 and 10:29. The gospel alone is the power of salvation for all who believe (Romans 1:16). The gospel is about God's free gift of grace. The gospel alone is what saves; no amount of our religious observance or relational feeling has the power to save.

Many of us are aware of how religion easily becomes a work, through legalistic observance of rules and rituals, but sometimes we forget that relationship can fall into the same traps. While the legalist chases adherence to the rules, the relationist chases the next feel-good moment. In this sense, relationship can become just another type of salvation by works among pietistic people who go from one passionate mountaintop experience to another, only to sour on God when he doesn't deliver according to the bargain they had struck. To put it another way, the problem with mere religion (religion as external duty) is that you end up with all structure, all bones, but no moving flesh, no flowing blood. It has the appearance of godliness, but there's no *life* there. But the problem with "mere relationship" spirituality is that it tries to find life in a shapeless, mushy form. Left to itself, flesh doesn't give life any more than dry bones do! While the bones don't give life, they provide the necessary structure for life to thrive. Without it, you end up with vapid, shallow, short-lived emotionalism.

Christianity is a religion. To say otherwise ignores Scripture and breaks congruity with billions of Christians from around the world and through 2,000 years of history. Christianity is a relationship. Many relational words are used to describe God and his people. He is our father, and we are his children. We know him. He speaks, and we listen. We are meant to constantly relate to our personal God. Christianity is expressed and experienced in both religion and relationship. But it's not *about* either.

Whether it be religion, relationship, or some other expression of our faith, faithful ministry doesn't let anything threaten the central place of the gospel. We are meant to be grounded in the life-giving roots of the gospel, which is not merely an initiation for new converts, but the foundation for everyone. The gospel—in all its depth, riches, and fullness—is repeatedly proclaimed to believer and unbeliever, churched and unchurched alike.

Shift #2: From Building a Large Group to Reaching a Large Campus

Where do many college ministries spend the greatest amount of time, energy, and resources? Generally, it's on the weekly large group meetings, complete with polished worship teams, fun activities, and funny emcees—all arranged to attract a good crowd. While this isn't all bad, and I'm not advocating doing away with these events and meetings entirely, they cannot be our sole or even primary focus. We need to shift from attracting a large group to reaching a large campus. We need to invest our time, energy, and resources in comprehensive campus-saturating strategies because let's be honest: as good as our programs are, there are *huge* segments of the campus population we will never see at our weekly large group meetings.

What we really need is a perspective shift: "So from now on we regard no one from a worldly point of view" (2 Corinthians 5:16). Our missional identity changes our point of view, particularly in how we view the non-Christians around us. It changes how we perceive our gatherings so we view them as the coming together of God's people on mission rather than a place or event. Dan Kimball explains this shift well: "If the church has become the place instead of the people on a mission, leaders only naturally start focusing their efforts on what people experience when they come to the place on Sundays"[1] (or whatever day of the week you meet).

Shift #3: From Head Counting to Seed Spreading

The missional approach also changes our perception of success and how we measure it. And to be honest, it complicates things. Traditionally, our metric of success has been pretty simple: "How many people are you getting?" We look at our head counts as the source of our success and legitimacy.

A missional approach knows things aren't as simple as this. What are a few hundred people among 40,000? What are fifty people among 5,000? The need is so much bigger, and fruitfulness will need to be measured by things other than weekly attendance. We should be figuring out ways to assess how well we're doing at discipling and equipping people for lifelong fruitfulness as missional Christians—on campus and beyond. We should be asking how many of the disciples we're making are then making disciples. We should be asking about both the quality and quantity of how we spread the gospel "seed." We all measure things, and we all keep score. But are we counting the right things?

Shift #4: From "Bible Studies/Small Groups" to Missional Communities

For years, we've gathered students for Bible studies, small groups, community groups, or an endless number of other names. Whatever we call them, many have one thing in common: they are clearly geared for Christians, whether it is stated explicitly or implicitly. But it's no longer okay to gather only Christian students in groups *merely* to focus on Bible knowledge and prayer requests. These elements should be part of your ministry, but if your group meetings don't act as a means of equipping students for mission, you're better off not having them because you're not discipling them for a life of mission.

Instead, we need missional communities—groups of students who share a burden for a particular people group and come together for the shared purpose of reaching that group together. They come together in community to preach the gospel to themselves and to help each other share it with others. They come together for prayer, encouragement, and equipping. They come together to model the kind of community into which they're inviting others.

These groups work best when their students are seeking to reach the people they already live, work, and study with all the time: engineers reaching engineers, athletes reaching athletes, honors students reaching honors students. But we also need students who will engage students who are different from them: the partying kids, the LGBTA community, the atheist-agnostic community, Muslims, and so on. Your campus has no shortage of unreached (or barely reached) people groups. A network of gospel-centered, mission-driven, student-led missional communities is the best way to saturate your campus with the knowledge of God. We'll talk much more about this in our chapters on discipleship.

Shift #5: From Assumptions About Students to Personal Knowledge of Students

Missional college ministry works hard to understand the people we seek to reach, but we must first ask ourselves, Who *are* we trying to reach, anyway? If you have never spent hours on your school's website viewing all the demographic data that is publicly available, you have more work to do. If you have never struck up random conversations in the student union building with your only agenda being to listen and learn, put this book down and get to work.

Jesus became a human being in order to save human beings. In the same way, our ministry needs to be incarnational. We need to spend the time listening to and learning about the people we have come to serve. Can you answer, off the top of your head, questions like the following?

- What's the racial/ethnic breakdown?
- How many students receive financial aid?
- How many have jobs?
- How many are from in state versus out of state?
- What are the most popular majors?
- How big is the Greek system?
- What percentage graduate in four years?
- Did our football/basketball team have a good season? Do people care?

Statistics aren't sufficient though. We must work hard to figure out how to engage the legions of students who will never walk through the doors of our large group meetings. Too much of campus ministry is spent talking *about* the unchurched/dechurched rather than talking *with* them. My ministry at Penn State has featured a weekly forum for skeptics of all types to question faith and doubt as well as some missional communities (whose leaders I disciple) that are designed to engage any and all questions that non-Christians may bring.

My time spent listening to many students has given me another set of questions (and some answers). I share these questions here to help you start thinking about your own school:

- How many students are involved in evangelical fellowships or churches on a regular basis?
- To what cultural idols are students expected to "bow down" at your school?
- What are the "temples of worship?"
- What are students passionate about?
- What shapes the religious/spiritual conversations on campus?
- What are the dominant spiritual attitudes on campus?

We must continually ask, What does it look like to communicate and incarnate the gospel in this particular place, at this particular time, to this particular people?

Shift #6: From Presumptions About Presence on Campus to Understanding and Blessing Our Campus

Missional college ministry works hard to understand our context of Higher Ed/academia. This is arguably both more difficult and more important than knowing our students. Most campus ministers are very relational people, so getting to know people comes relatively easy to us. Institutions? Not so much. But particular students come and go; universities remain. Traditional college ministers can work on a campus for many years reaching students without having much interest in redeeming and renewing places and institutions. This is a tragedy. Too many campus ministries barely seek to understand the campuses where they minister, let alone the larger context in which their campuses exist.

Where our ministry is located is not an irrelevant or extraneous detail. Each campus, and each city or community in which it is located, is unique. Ministry to, and by, these campus communities must be shaped by context. We should be asking, What is it about Higher Ed that makes it a particularly challenging, strategic, and exciting mission field? What are the institutional, social, and cultural obstacles to the gospel here? What would this sector of society look like if it were increasingly renewed by the gospel?

We need to stop complaining about our campuses. We need to remember that it is a privilege for us to be there. We need to stop venting about how our campuses are so liberal, or secular, or relativist, or postmodern. Rather, missional campus ministry believes that God has brought us and our students to this particular campus and community so we can learn about them and minister effectively in them.

Shift #7: From Talking *at* People to Talking *with* Them

Instead of arguing or retreating, we must engage people where they are. We must be willing to discuss and respond to the common objections to the gospel. Part of knowing our students and our context requires listening. Listen well, and you should start piecing together the objections that regularly combine to make Christianity seem unbelievable to non-Christians. On many campuses, these include several common charges: Christians are intolerant, Jesus can't be the only way, the Bible is historically unreliable, other religions have equal merit and they're all similar so choosing one isn't necessary, Christians are all right-wing conservatives, and others.

Missional ministry takes these objections seriously and humbly interacts with those who hold them. These objections will not be addressed through shrill debates but through respectful dialogue. Missionally speaking, it is best to not address the objections when only Christians or only non-Christians are present, but rather to simultaneously engage both groups. Doing so communicates to unbelievers that we are listening and models to believers how to engage in these conversations in informed, winsome, courageous, and most of all, *loving* ways.

Shift #8: From Evangelism as Merely a Program or Activity to a Holistic Way of Life

In the campus setting, students regard canned, impersonal evangelistic campaigns as ineffective and as reinforcing the objections they hold against Christianity. As a result, many Christians on campus (even ministers) rarely, if ever, share the gospel. Missional evangelism reunites deeds of mercy and justice with the verbal proclamation of the gospel as signs of the kingdom. An excellent example is the many unbelieving students who joined ministries such as Campus Crusade for Katrina relief. The context of mercy and justice becomes an appropriate and authentic arena for sharing the faith.

But sharing the faith verbally remains absolutely *essential.* Actions without words are unintelligible. If you do good deeds silently, people will think you are a good person. If you do them "in Jesus' name," they will (at least) think Jesus is good and want to find out more. At the same time, talk is cheap, but talk with action is incredibly powerful. As Tim Keller states, missional ministry

> must be more deeply and practically committed to deeds of compassion and social justice than traditional liberal churches and more deeply and practically committed to evangelism and conversion than traditional fundamentalist churches. This kind of church is profoundly "counter-intuitive" to American observers. It breaks their ability to categorize (and dismiss) it as liberal or conservative. Only this kind of church has any chance in the non-Christian west.[2]

Shift #9: From Insider Culture to Open and Comprehensible

Missional ministries should be known for their openness. We can start with the language we speak. In all of our communications, we should speak in a language that the unchurched can understand. Because we don't live in Christendom anymore, we can't assume that people are fluent in "Christianese." Terms must constantly be explained. This doesn't mean watering down the gospel. Rather, great effort and care are taken to speak faithfully about spiritual things in ways non-churched people can understand. There is a constant stream of translation to a foreign culture.

Missional speakers do not assume they are reminding people of what they already know but that they are explaining new things to them. In every meeting, every event, every setting, they always assume that unbelievers are present with them, people who are likely biblically illiterate and whose own faith is composed of a hodgepodge of spiritual ideas. Even basic concepts such as faith, grace, and sin have been compromised and dismissed by culture.

This is important in setting the tone for Christians as well because it models to them how to speak with unbelievers while also encouraging them to invite their friends, neighbors, and coworkers into the Christian community. As Keller notes, "If you speak and discourse as if your whole neighborhood is present (not just scattered Christians), eventually more and more of your neighborhood will find their way in or be invited."[3] Since we recognize that the Church has lost its place of privilege in society, we embrace our outsider status.

In our words and deeds, we can regain our prophetic role to speak out against injustice and abuse of privilege in those institutions that remain in power. The motive for working hard at changing our language is not marketing, but love for our neighbor. It is the expression of our willingness to do anything and change anything—even dearly loved traditions or practices—so that some would be saved.

Shift #10: From Acquiescing to the Postmodern Relegation of Faith to One Compartment of the Inner Life to Full-Life Engagement

Many campus ministries believe they are adequately equipping students to live out their faith. However, too many of us focus on things like private spiritual disciplines (such as praying and studying the Bible), and some evangelism. While we must teach our students these disciplines, missional campus ministry realizes that for students to take part in Christ's mission during college and beyond, they must be equipped to think and live Christianly in *every* sphere of life. As people on mission to Higher Ed, we intentionally and rigorously develop the intellect. This means calling students to whole person transformation—mind, body, and spirit—through the gospel, a transformation that begins through the renewing of their minds (Romans 12:2).

Missional campus ministry constantly helps students make sense of their lives from a deeply Christian perspective. Which cultural practices may be received because of common grace? Which must be rejected as clearly in opposition to the gospel? And which must be redeemed? Students are helped to view sex, relationships, work, school, money, entertainment, partying, alcohol, justice—and many other issues—from this Christian perspective.

Missional outreach is familiar with and engages the various "gospels" proclaimed in culture, particularly through movies, music, TV, and the internet. Because all truth is God's truth, many points of contact exist in popular culture—points that provide ample opportunities to connect people's experience with the gospel story. This takes wisdom and discernment, as well as a deep awareness (and appreciation) of both the biblical (meta)narrative and the cultural narratives. Being aware of the gospel story empowers us to engage the false gospels of our culture with the genuine article, which in turn exposes the counterfeits.

My hope is that you will examine what you're currently doing (or not doing) and make the shift to a more thoroughly missional ministry. And I hope that churches—whether you are currently reaching college students or not—will place a greater emphasis on intentionally reaching this crucial people group. The future health and vitality of the church in North America will depend on it.

Chapter 4
THE VIRTUES OF BEING THE "VISITING TEAM"

No recovery of the true wholeness of the Church's
nature is possible without a recovery of its
radically missionary character.[1]

—Lesslie Newbigin

Up in the Air is a movie that stars George Clooney as a traveling business-man whose job is firing people. He's utterly and intentionally rootless, a real tumbleweed who spends over 300 days a year away from home—so much so that during the film he reaches *ten million* miles in the air. On the side, he's a motivational speaker who espouses his life philosophy of having no attachments, no possessions, no relationships, and no baggage, which he calls the "empty backpack." The question the movie poses is whether an empty backpack leads to an empty life.

Most of us would—I hope—disagree with Clooney's character's philosophy. Yet it struck me that many Christians have a Christianized version of his life philosophy, one that often gets promoted among our students on campus:

> *We're just passing through.*
>
> *This world is not our home.*
>
> *It's all destined for destruction anyway.*
>
> *We're just pilgrims, aliens, strangers.*

This is the most dangerous kind of lie—partial truths using biblical language. But God has bigger purposes for us than to simply pass through our campuses, our lives, with an empty backpack.

Tempted to Disengage

Given the pressures and rampant idolatry on our campuses, it's understandable why we might want to disengage from campus culture. It was also a temptation for the original recipients of the letter written to the exiles in Babylon, which is found in Jeremiah 29. The context for this letter is important. The Jews are in exile after being conquered by the Babylonians. The best and brightest have been brought to Babylon, where they will spend the next seventy years. Being there is a constant reminder of their pain, their shame, their sorrow, and their punishment. They are subject to their hated enemies, who conquered them, killed their relatives, and desecrated the temple. They are living amid an idolatrous society with many corrupting influences. They probably expect God to tell them to hole up in a bunker somewhere. Instead, God has some surprising things to say (to us too) through Jeremiah.

The first thing God does is remind them that he's still sovereign and that he "carried" them there (Jeremiah 29:4). God put them there for a reason—and it's not to sit there looking at the calendar, waiting for their seventy years to be up. God says, "Yes, you are aliens and strangers in Babylon, but I want you to live as locals, as long-term residents. Yes, they are a pagan, idolatrous, hostile culture, but I don't want you to treat them as your enemies." Babylon was very far from God. In that sense, it was similar to our current campus cultures.

Your campus is a mission field, and that makes you a missionary. We are called to be part of God's redemptive plan in that place. We can't look at college as a rest stop on the way to rest of our lives. God wants us to engage our mission field. This statement has some huge implications for students, including this one that parents may not like to hear: your education is just one part of why God brought you to your campus! Let's not miss one of the most obvious facts about the Jews being in Babylon: they were vastly outnumbered in a foreign land. We could say they were the "visiting team."

The Virtues of Being the Visiting Team

Penn State has seven or even eight home football games almost every year. Most colleges can't schedule this way, but Penn State is one of the few that can. Why is this? Penn State Football is a privileged, storied, and powerful program that, as a result, has an insatiable demand for tickets and possesses one of the largest stadiums and the largest alumni association in the country. Each home game is incredibly lucrative, and they have no problem lining up teams to accept a nice payout in return for being annihilated in front of 110,000+ adoring Nittany Lion fans. Penn State has teams come to them because they *can*.

Many campus ministries today act like we're Penn State when our situation isn't actually like that at all. Like the Jews in exile, we need to embrace our visiting team status. On the campus gridiron of ideas, we're not really competition. We're often an afterthought and tolerated with a condescending pat on the head. At worst, we're regarded as a threat to the institution and threatened with expulsion (as several high profile cases have documented). While we may have a few "upsets" here and there, in general we're not competitive, not admired, and worst of all—not even on the radar. In many places, we are irrelevant.

The absurdity of it all is that we keep acting like the home team, but we spend our energy running scrimmages for the faithful few to watch on our turf while not a lot is getting done. An exhibition game is fun in April, but who wants to watch that in October, November, or on New Year's Day? Campus ministries need to wake up. We need to accept that we are not in the place of power or privilege on most campuses. We need to embrace our status as the visiting team.

For example, I've been to some meetings of our campus atheist-agnostic club. I'm usually the only Christian present. Like many Christians, atheists feel they are a persecuted minority, but atheists are more accustomed to marginalization and stigma. Several of them make it a practice to visit different churches on Sunday mornings. I suppose they may be there to mock us and our beliefs and laugh among themselves, but the point is *they go*. They're willing to be the visiting team. Consequently, they are generally adept at articulating their beliefs and engaging with those who disagree with them.

In contrast, Christians are notorious for retreating to our bunkers rather than venturing onto someone else's turf. When we are willing to do so, we often find we're making some actual progress. At these atheist meetings, I've met new people and had great conversations with students who were intrigued I was there. I even invited several of them to my faith-and-doubt forum. Only one student seemed offended that I was there and had some harsh words for me. I'll go into any arena if that's all I have to deal with!

The point of missional, incarnational ministry is that we leave our comfort zones and *go* to people. We meet them where they are. I can think of at least three reasons why it's good to be the visiting team:

1. It's disarming. You can't possibly pull a power play if you're the only Christian in the room!
2. It shows your willingness to listen. In case you haven't noticed, that's one of the most common complaints people have about Christians.
3. It's what Jesus did: "He came to that which was his own, but his own did not receive him" (John 1:11).

Still, it's not enough to know that we're the visiting team on a mission field. We have to know how to live, work, and generally behave once we're there. We have to know how to engage the culture around us.

Cultural Engagement

Perhaps you've heard how Christians are meant to be "in but not of" the world, based on Jesus' prayer in John 17. For all our talk about in/not of, we haven't lived out this phrase very well. Christians have chosen several other approaches besides in/not of. We could place these different postures toward culture in the chart below. Each is a variation of being "in" or "of" a culture.

I.	II.
Accommodationist In and of Just like culture "Come to us— we're no different from you!"	Redemptive/Transformationalist In but not of Holy counterculture "We'll go to you."
III. Extractional Not in but of Subculture "Come to us."	IV. Fundamentalist Not in and not of Against culture "Go away!"

Quadrant I represents people both "in" and "of" the world. It is impossible to differentiate them from the culture at large because they look just like it. Their lives have no points of tension or friction with the current zeitgeist. This was the path taken by classic twentieth-century liberalism, and it's the path being taken by many in the Church today.

Let's move to the polar opposite, quadrant IV, "not in and not of." This was the path taken by early twentieth-century American fundamentalism. It's a form of Pharisaism, defining being good as the things you don't do. People who live this way take an oppositional, negative stance toward the world. Unfortunately, this spirit is alive and well in many circles.

Those in quadrant III seek to avoid the failures of quadrants I and IV but end up recycling mistakes from both. This quadrant represents the failure of much of the evangelical church in North America. Rather than engaging the larger world, people in this quadrant cut themselves off, but instead of being different, they create their own Christianized versions of everything the world has and does, expending enormous amounts of energy on a Christian subculture.

The Jews in Babylon would have been tempted to one of these options. Jeremiah 29 is a call to a quadrant II redemptive, transformational presence, an "in but not of" counterculture that faithfully engages the world around it.

Redemptive Engagement

To quadrant I accommodationist types, God reminds them that they belong to him. He promises that, though they are tempted to wander, he will bring them back when their hearts turn back to him. To quadrant IV fundamentalist types, those who would live in enmity and opposition to their surrounding culture, he says, "Seek the peace and prosperity of the city . . . pray to the LORD for it" (Jeremiah 29:7).

To quadrant III subculture types, God has the most to say. To those inclined to simply survive while passing through, he says, "Instead of living as if you're leaving tomorrow, I want you to settle down. Build houses. Plant gardens. Instead of doing things that benefit only you, bless the larger culture. Leave a mark on this place." It's a biblical principle: wherever God has put you, be *all the way* there. The ministry of presence is an underrated and dying art. With the advent of technology that promises to let us be everywhere at once, we're spread so thin that we don't impact the places in which we live and the people who live there with us. Obviously, I'm not saying students should apply Jeremiah 29 by building a literal house in the middle of the student union building, but dream and imagine what it would look like for the kingdom of God to come in power on your campus. Go beyond revival and ask what *redemption* would look like.

I ask my students to imagine what it would look like if God's shalom would come to our campus. What if God's peace and prosperity would come? When we get our holy imaginations going, we talk about less sexual assault. Less depression. Less deadening with drugs and alcohol and mindless sex. Less emptiness. In many ways, engaging our mission helps answer the perennial question of college students: "Why am I here?" Yes, the ultimate answer is to glorify God, to love him with all our heart, soul, mind, and strength. But how do you suppose that glorifying love gets worked out and expressed on a daily basis? By joining God in his mission.

More Than Survival

Unfortunately, our Christian high school students heading off to college have been told something different: they have been told—if not explicitly—that their goal in college is simply to survive with their faith intact, to make it through without falling into sin. In talking with many churched students, I've found that many have absorbed two false, unmissional assumptions. The first is that they are not *really* called to reach out to their world—just survive it. Outreach would be a nice bonus, but generally speaking, stay in your protective bubble as much as possible. Get good grades, don't get pregnant, and come home as often as possible with your nose clean. It's as if Jesus never said, "My prayer is not that you take them out of the world" (John 17:15) or "as the Father has sent me, I am sending you" (John 20:21).

The second is that they can be protected from the world by not behaving badly. But this idea isn't missional at all. In fact, it's Pharisaical. Jesus said it's not what goes into us that makes us unclean; it's what comes out of us (Matthew 15:11). "Don't do bad things" is not biblical; nor is it a compelling charge to give your high school graduates as they head off to the big, bad campus. No wonder so many bail on their faith!

Youth pastors and parents, I plead with you to give your high school-ers a bigger charge than that. How many churches commission their graduates as missionaries to their campuses? We should stick with Jesus' parting instructions: "go . . . make disciples . . . baptizing . . . teaching them to obey everything I commanded" (Matthew 28:19-20). That's much more compelling; that's a mission, a purpose bigger than ourselves.

God has put Christians on campus for a reason, and it's to do the good works he prepared for us in advance to do (Ephesians 2:10). For students, college should be a process of discovering who they are and what God has in store for them. College should be approached with the mindset that every Christian is called and sent to the world, just as Jesus was sent into the world. When students and ministers approach college through an in/not of faithful engagement posture, we are joining God in his mission, which is to restore God's peace or shalom to a fallen creation through his son Jesus Christ.

Missing the Mission

Every year I meet well-meaning students who have been taught that college is just something to survive while passing through—that the un-desirable aspects of college life are things from which to hide. These are the students whose faith I worry about most because people who miss God's purposes will eventually become detached, bored, and disengaged from God himself. Boredom and detachment are already common on our campuses, but it's a tragedy when Christians look as bored as their class-mates. We, of all people, should be passionate, engaged, and full of the life that Jesus promised in John 10:10. When we're bored and disengaged from God's purposes, we become susceptible to what "false prophets" are saying. Jeremiah warns us that we'll be tempted to listen to "dreams" and "lies" that are not from God (29:8-9). These lies are often Christian versions of false beliefs that are already well established in our culture.

Christian gnosticism is the belief that all that matters is what's "spiritu-al" or "going to heaven." The material, the physical, what's right in front of us—none of it ultimately matters. It's possible to be so heavenly minded as to be no earthly good. But as we see in the Lord's prayer, this isn't the kind of heavenly mindedness that Jesus taught.

We can also fall into Christian atheism, being so earthly-minded as to be no heavenly good. This is the case when we live as if this life is the only life we'll ever have. The dominant message today, which is easy to absorb, is that pleasure, comfort, security, safety, success, and achievement are the only things worth pursuing. Jesus says to seek first the kingdom—and trust him to take care of the rest.

Heavenly Minded *and* Earthly Good

Faithful quadrant II engagement will avoid the pseudo-spirituality of Christian gnosticism and the unabashed materialism of Christian atheism. It means that with the kingdom of heaven in mind, we seek the peace and prosperity of the city (or campus) where God has placed us. Heaven is seen not as "pie in the sky, by and by," nor as eternally playing harps in the clouds, but the kingdom of God come to bear on every aspect of our existence, the reign and rule of God. C. S. Lewis said,

> If you read history, you will find that the Christians who did most for the present world were just those who thought most of the next. The Apostles themselves, who set on foot the conversion of the Roman Empire, the great men who built up the Middle Ages, the English Evangelicals who abolished the Slave Trade, all left their mark on Earth, precisely because their minds were occupied with Heaven.[2]

In other words, Christians are people who leave their campus or city better than they found it. They are so deeply connected to Jesus and his mission that they can't help but bless those around them.

Redeeming Jeremiah 29:11

Being missionally minded should deliver us from individualistic, self-centered readings of Scripture, including the verse you already know from Jeremiah 29:11: "'For I know the plans I have for you,' declares the LORD, 'plans to prosper you and not to harm you, plans to give you hope and a future.'" This is possibly the most popular college student life verse of all time. It's a tremendously encouraging one to people trying to figure out their plans for the future at such a meaningful crossroads of their lives. But we've been abusing it. We need to redeem Jeremiah 29:11, the verse that's spawned innumerable bookmarks, mugs, Bible covers, fridge magnets, bumper stickers, and other Christian kitsch. We love this verse—but hear it in context! To discover God's plan, join him in his work of renewal. Hear it through the missional grid, in the context of the passage. The verse isn't about you; it's about God's kingdom agenda. You have a mission, a kingdom purpose.

Verse eleven is embedded in God's plan to bless the city. This means that college is fundamentally not a place to realize *our* plans and ambitions, but God's plan. Kingdom living changes our plans and priorities. It requires us to lay down our lives to bless, renew, and redeem God's creation.

Chapter 5

REDEMPTIVELY ENGAGING THE CAMPUS

Revolutions have always started with the young.

Students take on all sorts of identities when they arrive on campus: they become the intellectual bookworms, the lab rats, the dumb jocks, the party-hardy frat boys and sorority girls, the burned out stoners, the get-a-life gamers, the radical activists, the crazy Christians, and many more. Yes, all of these are stereotypes, but they are characters in the story of what people think "college" is supposed to be.

We have a different story to tell, the story of God's redemptive work in the world through Jesus Christ. Our part of the story is on campus. We don't passively accept the roles that others have for us; instead, we seek to love, serve, and bless the campus, in Jesus' name. But *how* do we do this? This chapter details some practical steps toward faithful, redemptive engagement.

1. Listen, *Really* Listen, to Them

First, we must listen. This is part of how we become genuinely incarnated among the people we seek to serve. Many pastors, including Tim Keller and Mark Driscoll, have written about the great amounts of time and energy they devoted to listening to all kinds of people in the early days of their ministries. If we listen well, what seems very time-intensive in the short-term will become a powerful backbone for future ministry.

This discipline should force us out of the Christian bubble because it requires us to visit groups, clubs, and organizations very different from ours. It means we should be devoting significant time to the process of learning and forming friendships that cross lines and allow for meaningful dialogue. Too many campus ministries don't seek to really listen to those on the campuses to which they have been called. They lack the authenticity and relevance that can come only through spending time listening. Unsurprisingly, as a result, their ministries are not and will not be effective over the long term.

I was reminded of this at the very first meeting of the faith and doubt forum I organized. One militant atheist named Yasic shared with the group that he owned seventeen copies of C. S. Lewis's *Mere Christianity*. He said that every year on his birthday, his Christian friends would give him a copy—thus his collection. I then asked him, "Did anyone ever read through it *with you?*" His response? "No."

As Christians, we've substituted books for relationships and one-sided discussions for genuine dialogue. Yasic and others ended up sticking around for our semester-long discussion we called The Sojourn Forum. My time with Yasic has also yielded some interesting conversations and insight into what he *really* thinks and believes as opposed to the caricature of a militant atheist he could easily become in my mind. One night he revealed to the group that, though he believes Christians are foolishly superstitious and might as well believe in the Tooth Fairy and the Easter Bunny, he still prays sometimes. He prays "God, if you're real, reveal yourself to me." I told Yasic I would join him in that prayer.

I've learned that without listening, without welcoming Yasic into our discussions and getting to know him, his thoughts, beliefs, and fears, I would have never known how to pray for him. And he wouldn't have seen a picture of Christianity that differs from the view of us he had—as a close-minded, foolish, superstitious group.

2. Develop a Heart for Your Campus

I remember listening to a *This American Life* podcast on Penn State called "#1 Party School." At one point the show went to a frat party and interviewed a guy and a girl who were both inebriated. The guy, with no inhibitions, despite having a microphone from a national radio show in front of him, proceeded to tell the girl, "I'm just trying to get you drunk right now so I can take advantage of you later." The girl's response? "That's so awkward." Awkward? Really? I can think of a lot of things to call that guy's words, but "awkward" doesn't even come close. That's someone's daughter!

Many times since hearing that podcast, I've wondered what happened to that girl that night. I've wondered why she would put herself in that kind of situation. I've wondered about the guy and what he is becoming. It breaks my heart to think of the thousands of girls who downplay jokes about being sexually assaulted and the brokenness that is not only tolerated but celebrated on our campuses.

I don't believe you can really engage a campus you don't care about. We need a burden, a heart for our mission field. We need a heart to see them differently—not from a "worldly point of view," but as Jesus sees them. If I didn't have a heart for my campus, I'd probably roll my eyes at those fraternity boys and sorority girls and their lifestyles. Instead, I'm burdened for them. Jesus has given me the gift of weeping for them like he wept over Jerusalem because they're "like sheep without a shepherd."

3. Pray

Jeremiah knew that the Jews would not be able to redemptively and faithfully engage their context if they didn't pray for their ability to do so. It's the same throughout church history and college ministry. You simply can't find a great movement of God that doesn't involve prayer. From the Great Awakening of George Whitefield, Jonathan Edwards, and the Wesleys in the 1730s and 1740s to the ministry of evangelist Dwight Moody and the birth of the Student Volunteer Movement in the late 1800s—from the ministry of evangelist Billy Graham and the birth of campus ministries like Campus Crusade for Christ, InterVarsity, and the Navigators in the middle of the twentieth century to the occasional revivals that spring up on college campuses today, one thing always precedes campus transformation: *God's people pray!*

4. Bless—Seek Peace and Prosperity

When you look at the vision and mission of your ministry, do you make it an explicit goal to bless the university, to make it a better place? How many of us truly seek the peace and prosperity of the campus on which God has placed us rather than simply building our own organizations? We should be asking what would make the campus a better place and how we can be part of that change. What would make students, faculty, and administration say, "I may not agree with you on everything, but I'm sure glad you're here?" If your ministry no longer existed tomorrow, would anyone notice? More than that, would they care? Would anything be different? An honest assessment of our answers to these questions should lead to deeper reflection on what it means to bless our campuses.

5. Teach That It's All Spiritual

It's not uncommon in college ministry to give students the impression that it's only the "spiritual" stuff that matters: reading your Bible, praying, showing up to fellowship meetings and church, and the like. Implicitly and sometimes explicitly, students hear the message that everything else—the studying and extracurriculars and weekend activities—is *not* spiritual. The results of this unbiblical dualism are devastating. Students predisposed to forming Christian cliques focus on fellowship groups and are cut off from any real engagement with the rest of campus while others do whatever they want to do when not in church and look like any other students except for a few hours per week. Neither group is engaging their campus redemptively—and neither is living missionally.

We need to help students see everything as spiritual, to help them view their studies, their sports, their clubs, and everything else as belonging to God and as part of their offering to him. Simultaneously, we don't view our ministries as just another extracurricular activity. Rather, we emphasize that we are a "co-curricular" group—one that helps students make sense of God's comprehensive call on their lives in *every* aspect of life.

6. Go on Mission Together

The early church is famous for the richness of community. For instance, we sometimes fail to remember that the book of Jeremiah was written to a community, a people, the gathered exiles in Babylon. Daniel and his three friends were part of this group and formed a "missional community" within it. Even Jesus did not go it alone but gathered disciples around him.

Mission is inextricably connected to our gospel-shaped, countercultural, transformative communities. When we gather to love God and love one another, God goes with us to love our neighbors. It's easier to engage people who are different from us when we don't go it alone. We'll talk much more about this in the chapters on evangelism and discipleship.

7. Raise the Bar

Because we minister to college students, it is imperative that we strive to establish and maintain a trained and learned campus ministry. If we're not familiar with the intellectual climate of our day, and particularly the intellectual arguments for and against the faith, we are not truly engaging our contexts. We must be all things to all people, so that we might save some (see 1 Corinthians 9:19-23).

John Stackhouse is on faculty at Regent College in Vancouver. His post called "Engaging the University: The Vocation of Campus Ministry" is a must-read for anyone in the field. It is a stinging rebuke, but one we need to hear:

Many campus staff—and leaders on up the hierarchy of campus or-ganizations—have only an undergraduate degree, and often in a field that prepares them badly for ideological contest and Christian disci-ple-making (e.g., engineering, natural sciences, commerce, medicine). More recently, more have a master's degree or better in a relevant field. But one wonders why such qualifications are not simply re-quired, the way denominations and congregations require at least one theological degree to do the job? What is this job that requires so little theological training, so little philosophical awareness?

What one sees too much of in campus ministry instead is an ar-rogant amateurism. *We'll do it ourselves. . . .*

We staff don't need advanced training in theology or Christian discipleship; furthermore, we'll set up our own study centres and do the teaching ourselves rather than work with schools that already ex-ist who have much better-trained faculty. The history of these move-ments shows that some staff will even innovate theologically and teach ideas that they enjoy thinking are "cutting-edge," while what they breathlessly announce as "fresh" is simply the latest version of an old heresy that any genuine theological expert could spot at 100 metres. The intellect needs valuing better than this. . . .

Similarly, one finds precious little involvement of the people who know the university best: not students, not alumni, not staffers of Christian groups, but professors and administrators, who inhabit and who shape the university far more than any other participants in it. To ignore them so consistently, which most student missions do at every level, is to try to work at a hospital without consulting physicians or nurses or administrators, or to work in a law courts building without consulting judges, lawyers, or police officers.[1]

You may be offended by this statement, but before rejecting Stackhouse, ask yourself, Where is this true in my organization and in my ministry? Is there anything *less* missional than being intellectually uninformed and shallow in the world of Higher Ed? In what ways might this uninformed "arrogant amateurism" be holding us back from accomplishing our mission? Ask yourself this question: Who else in Higher Ed is accepted for being less than learned and accomplished in their field? So why is it acceptable for us?

8. Equip Students

Rather than being passive consumers of ministry, students are called to jump in with the same missional charge. They make the best campus missionaries. After all, they're the ones who join the clubs, sit in the classes, play on the teams, and lead student government. They're the ones who get to have the deep conversations at 2:00 a.m. in the dorm when someone pours their heart out. In contrast, ministry staff are, by virtue of our role, age, and stage in life, removed from many of these settings. The staff calling is to equip the saints. It's not our job to *do* the ministry; it's our job to help students lead and do the ministry.

Avoiding the errors of subculture, cultural accommodation, and cultural opposition, missional students and staff allow the truths of the gospel to seep down into every area of life. We model faithful engagement with the "stuff" of college. This means radical departures from dominant approaches to sex, money, power, school and work, and entertainment.

Christians recognize all of these as gifts but in the freedom of the gospel seek to neither abuse nor idolize them the way the culture does. It will definitely mean standing out on our campuses! But standing out can raise another question.

"How Far Is Too Far?"

If you're like me, you associate this question with sexual/relational boundaries. It's still a common question among Christian students, but I'm also hearing it come up in missional contexts. There's no doubt that living missionally moves us into all kinds of challenges to be faithful. We're leaning into the tension. Just as Jesus faced temptation in the desert at the beginning of his ministry, so will we. Temptations are real and must be discussed. Oftentimes, we entertain a temptation by trying to fool ourselves (and others) by asking questions that sound pious but are really a smokescreen to allow us to act out sinfully.

As with the sexual version of "How far is too far?" students seem to be asking, "How much can I get away with?" Whatever the scenario, I usually question their motives when I hear this question. They ask, "If I'm trying to reach people who party, I guess that means I have to drink, right? And I should probably have more than one drink so I don't look lame, right? 'All things to all people,' right?"

As with the sexual version of this line of questioning, the point is not to hammer out the *exact* point at which one goes "too far." Trying to do so only leads to legalism. Instead, we should come back to motives. I talk to my students about how "too far" is when you are worshiping the idols of pleasure or other people's approval more than Jesus. "Too far" is when you are putting fun or getting someone to like you ahead of your mission. "How far is too far?" is the wrong question because it's not focusing on the mission. Instead, we should ask, How can I glorify God tonight? What would be most honoring to him?

"But I'm Only in College!"

The objection we often hear from students is "I'm only in college." This is another way of saying, "You can't expect much from me." And students are using this excuse for more than ministry and faith. Sociologists have noticed that the adolescence that used to be confined to college now seems to extend all the way through the twenties. Some experts are calling this a new, distinct life stage called "emerging adulthood." Not teenagers but not yet adults. Not fully dependent but not fully responsible either.[2] The Amish give their young people a season called *rumspringa* in which they are free to throw off all restraints and go a little crazy. Today, it seems that many people in their twenties and even thirties are on an extended rumspringa.

But God's calendar doesn't recognize rumspringa. Our message to students is this: Your life starts now! From generation to generation, the young have changed the world. Excuses about youth don't hold much weight with God. Just look at how he deals with Jeremiah's objections:

"Ah, Sovereign LORD," I said, "I do not know how to speak; I am only a child." But the LORD said to me, "Do not say, 'I am only a child.' You must go to everyone I send you to and say whatever I command you. Do not be afraid of them, for I am with you and will rescue you," declares the LORD. (Jeremiah 1:6-8)

Remember also Paul's command to Timothy: "Don't let anyone look down on you because you are young, but set an example for the believers in speech, in life, in love, in faith and in purity" (1 Timothy 4:12). Paul believes that youth is not the same as immaturity. Therefore, youth does not disqualify people from leading. Those who are young and able should look for opportunities to serve and lead—and we must allow and encourage them to do so when they are willing.

Alliance Christian Fellowship at Penn State is a student church that has existed for over forty years and still has a strong presence today. A few years ago, they tackled a project that many established churches would have found intimidating. They not only adopted an orphanage in Peru, but they also took charge of building it—to the tune of $130,000, which their students and alumni raised! They sent teams down to do the construction every spring, summer, and winter break, and a graduate student in architecture took charge of designing it. The work of students has very literally transformed the lives of the children in that orphanage, but more importantly it has served as a concrete example of Christ's love to those in that Peruvian community as well as their own.

Revolutions Start with the Young

Revolutions have always started with the young. We see this countless times throughout the Bible. God didn't speak to the high priest Eli; he spoke to the boy Samuel. It wasn't King Saul but the boy David who killed Goliath. It wasn't the wicked Kings Manasseh and Amon who reformed Judah; it was the eight-year-old King Josiah. And let's not forget that Jesus was in his early thirties when the older Nicodemus, "the teacher of Israel," came to him. It wasn't the older Pharisees and teachers of the law who supported and followed Jesus—in fact, they were the ones who took the most shots at him. It's the same today for those who are full of zeal and want to faithfully follow Jesus. A missional revolution that could change the world can start today on our college campuses.

Part Two

GROWING
THE MISSION
EVANGELISM,
DISCIPLESHIP, AND
LEADERSHIP

Chapter 6
HANGING OUT ON MARS HILL

New people, cultures, and ideas
call for new approaches to
sharing our faith.

It may seem a bit strange to devote an entire chapter to evangelism in a book on missional college ministry. After all, having a missional orientation to life and ministry means we do away with modern or Christendom-era compartmentalization of the Christian life and proclaim the good news in everything we do, right? Evangelism isn't something we do; rather, it flows from who we are. It's not an activity we can schedule but something that should be happening continually.

Previous generations "did evangelism" through mass communication techniques such as inviting friends to a preaching crusade like Billy Graham's or by blanketing a school or beach with tracts such as Campus Crusade's "Four Spiritual Laws" and "Knowing God Personally." These approaches have led many, many people to faith in Christ over the years. But by focusing on reaching the masses, this kind of evangelism deemphasized the relational component of sharing the gospel. Too often, those being evangelized were treated as if they all looked the same—with the same worldviews, same questions, and same desires. In the wrong hands, these tools became crutches instead.

Reaching Our Friends

Many of us don't turn to those tools today. We're fairly pragmatic and have grown suspicious of foolproof techniques and impersonal approaches. We doubt—with good reason—that approaching strangers with tracts or even clever napkin sketches will yield much good fruit. In response, we've swung to the other side of the pendulum: we talk about friendship and relational evangelism.

"Friendship" and "relational" aren't bad, but these words have been used to form excuses for downplaying actual evangelism. We make the unbiblical assumptions that we can't share the gospel with someone who isn't relationally close to us and that it takes a long time to get there. It's clear though from the story of Zacchaeus, the woman at the well in John 4, and many others that Jesus did not approach evangelism this way. While relationship is certainly a powerful medium for sharing the gospel, relational evangelism in which we don't bring up Jesus isn't evangelism. It may qualify as outreach, but it is not evangelism because the good news is not being proclaimed.

Service Evangelism

Just as evangelism is not equivalent to throwing tracts at strangers or building friendships in which we never speak about Christ, neither is it equivalent to being a good person, doing acts of service, or being socially conscious. If I give blood, recycle, feed the homeless, and collect money for disaster relief, people will assume *I'm* a good person. That's not the gospel. It's actually the worst kind of idolatry because it elevates me instead of Christ. But if I serve in Jesus' name, then I may have an opportunity to give the reason for the hope that I have and to share the gospel.

Our resistance to proclaim our faith in Christ in a tolerant age means that we evangelicals have gone soft on evangelism. We who claim to believe the good news seem disinterested in sharing it with others. Someone would have to hit us over the head with a cast iron frying pan, asking, "How can I be saved?" for us to share the gospel with them. While evangelism has never been easy or popular, it's always been an essential part of following Jesus. So when it comes to our own qualms about evangelism, we need to distinguish between 1) the call and command to evangelize and 2) the culturally appropriate, biblically faithful modes of evangelizing. The first will stand until Jesus comes again and does not change, but the second is *always* changing. New people, cultures, and ideas call for new approaches to sharing our faith.

Once we've repented of our fears and pledged our obedience to Jesus' commands, we can take a hard, thoughtful look at how evangelism is done. Sharing the good news of Jesus can't be reduced to techniques. Nor is it about fluffy, fanciful "friendship evangelism" that never actually evangelizes. It's about serious, purposeful, provocative engagement with people who don't know Jesus. It's about having a faith that compels and literally provokes (calls forth) a response.

Up on Mars Hill

In Acts 17:16-34, we read about Paul's visit to Mars Hill, or the Areopagus, in Athens. This is the place where the Athenians spent their time "doing nothing but talking about and listening to the latest ideas" (verse 21). Sometimes missed in this passage is that Paul's preaching starts in the synagogue and the *agora*, or marketplace. It's on the basis of his provocative evangelizing among religious types and in the marketplace that he's invited to the more exclusive, culturally distant Mars Hill in the first place.

Once there, Paul knows what to do. He changes his approach and, before "preaching the good news about Jesus and the resurrection" (verse 18), he quotes their poets (their culture) as a means to engage them. He shows a deep knowledge of and sensitivity to their culture as well as a willingness to change his methods to help his audience hear the message. And how is he received? Some people mock him; others want to hear more, and some people are saved. This passage has served as something of a template for Christian engagement of culture, and two of the largest, most influential churches in the U.S. take their name from it.

Some people read Paul's Mars Hill encounter a bit differently from the way I do. They see it as Paul's least effective ministry endeavor, even as a negative example. Their discomfort with Acts 17 is this: not many people come to faith. (Though Paul's day at Mars Hill would still be a *really good day* for most of us, right?) But Acts tells us the story of how the gospel went to everyone and everywhere in the known world, so in that sense Paul's time on Mars Hill is part of the success story.

As someone who spends a good time up on the Mars Hill of my campus with students who like to debate all the latest ideas (Acts 17:21), I'm keenly aware of the challenges Paul faced. One aspect of my calling there has been to minister to the militant atheists, agnostics, and pagans on campus. It's a challenge to redemptively engage with them, particularly during the last couple years when the New Atheist movement has been throwing its weight around. I think stories like Mars Hill cause us to reevaluate our grid of what constitutes success. Not every day will be Pentecost, and Paul never gets the "instant" results like Peter does, but that certainly doesn't make him a failure.

Seeing Your Campus on the Continuum

I've been helped in my thinking on this by missiologist Ralph Winter's scale for illustrating "cultural distance" from the gospel, as mediated and adapted by Alan Hirsch in *The Forgotten Ways* and elsewhere.[1] Imagine placing everyone on a continuum, ranging from "m0," which would be little to no cultural distance from the gospel, all the way to "m4," which would be huge cultural, racial, ethnic, religious, and sociological obstacles, such as a devoted Muslim in Saudi Arabia.

At Penn State, we estimate that out of 44,000 total students, approximately 1,500 students are actively engaged in evangelical ministries. The vast majority of these students fall into the m0 or m1 crowd. Consequently, despite our best and stated intentions, a large number of ministries are competing for a very small percentage of students. So, what about those who fall into the m2, m3, and m4 groupings? It's not an exaggeration to say that only 10 percent of overall ministry efforts and resources on our campus are used to reach the other 90 percent of the student population. If the overall college student population weren't at an all-time high, we'd be experiencing considerable declines in our numbers—and I'm sure we wouldn't be happy about that. As it is, we're somewhat passive.

Reaching the People Groups on Campus

Christians tend to see the campus in black-and-white terms—the Christians and the non-Christians. While this distinction is of eternal significance, it is not the only relevant distinction. I believe that in order to be more effective college ministers, we should view our campuses the way missionaries view their contexts. Not only should we see college students in general as a people group—and an incredibly strategic one at that—but each of our campuses contains hundreds of people groups.

In the typical college movie, we generally see only a handful of groups on campus: jocks, nerds, Greeks, and stoners. But students identify themselves using a number of factors: race and ethnicity, major, hobbies, sports, sexuality, religion, and hometown, among others. Penn State has over 900 student groups, which include fraternities and sororities, service organizations, clubs for all different majors, for those who love anime and manga, film, astronomy, caving, ballroom dancing, snowboarding, and so many others. And these are just the official clubs and organizations! If we were painting the campus, we wouldn't use only one color—we would use hundreds—which is why we need many approaches and many laborers to reach many people groups.

Tim Keller wrote an influential article called "Ministry in the New Global Culture of Major City-Centers."[2] In it, he argues that we must understand the worldviews of those to whom we minister, and that the categories of "modern vs. postmodern" are insufficient. He identifies four common worldviews present in major city centers: traditionalists, moderns, postmoderns, and "transmoderns" or post-postmoderns. While we don't have space here to adequately discuss the differences between these groups and the implications for ministry, it's imperative to realize that in our current contexts, ministry can't be reduced to either/or, black-and-white categories. The multifactorial complexity of our field means that effective ministry requires a great deal of sensitivity and discernment.

I know many defenders of more "old school" evangelistic approaches who assure me that their tracts still work. And I'm sure they're right: those approaches certainly work for people who are wired to respond to that particular mode (generally, these people are traditional and modern thinking in their worldview). But just because these modes work now doesn't mean they will continue to work. And one-size-fits-all outreach and evangelism will *not* work when we're trying to reach an entire campus.

Our culture is incredibly fragmented and becoming more that way. The sociological word for this change is "microheterogenization"—the proliferation of many, many fractured subgroups of people. One way to better engage our campuses is to work toward determining where our students fall on the cultural distance/openness spectrum. How open are they to Christianity? What does the scale look like on your campus? In talking to my students about spiritual openness on campus, including some recent converts, we've adapted the scale for our campus population. Our adapted scale is below in case you'd like to use it for your own campus:

m0: Those already in the Christian fold or actively looking; favorably disposed, open people (churched, professing Christians or on the verge). They are the ones who would show up regardless.

m1: Perhaps churched but disaffected. Or actively spiritual, not necessarily religious. They're on the fence. They have spiritual questions on their minds and are open-minded, not closed. Willing to give it a shot. Nominal Christians or friendly non-Christians.

m2: The generally silent, apathetic-toward-Christianity group. This group is likely the majority, larger than the other groups combined. They come across as if they couldn't care less. While they might be willing to listen, they generally find religious conversations to be shrill, obnoxious, and irrelevant. If you bring up these topics, they shrug their shoulders and say, "Meh."

m3: Suspicious, skeptical, perhaps reacting to negative examples within the church, but might be willing to give you an audience.

m4: Active in beliefs or religions very negative to Christianity, even antagonistic. For example, some (though not all) militant atheists or hard-line Muslims.

Many campus ministers I know report a similar breakdown on their campuses as well, and we have some support from scientific studies. According to research conducted by Christian Smith in the book *Souls in Transition*, fewer than 1 percent of emerging adults between ages eighteen and twenty-three are regularly attending a religious meeting other than church.[3] The majority of emerging adults are indifferent to religion. And according to research by the Pew Research Center, millennials (those born after 1980) are less religiously affiliated, attend worship less often, and fewer of them than any previous generation think religion is "very important."[4]

Defining Missional Success

In our current contexts, how can we determine whether we're ministering effectively? This is a crucial question going forward. What constitutes success for Paul at Mars Hill, and throughout Acts, is that he is able to penetrate any and every people group that he comes across, no matter how far they are from the gospel. If Paul ever crunches the numbers, he's not counting heads so much as counting churches he's established and people groups he's reached. He's looking forward to the day when "people from every tribe, tongue and nation" are at the throne.

Because we're coming out of a Christendom era that was characterized by a Christian-friendly cultural consensus, our attitudes and expectations about evangelism have been shaped by doing ministry among those who are not far off, who reside in the m0 or m1 zone. We have inferred that because these people make on-the-spot decisions to receive Christ, conversion is an event and one that can be reached in a matter of minutes. But this belief ignores all the preparatory work of the cultural environment, which we discussed in chapter one. Conversion has always been a process—it just didn't appear that way in our Christendom context and among m0 and m1 types. Many people still have a conversion "moment," but those moments are preceded by a great deal of conversations, relationships, thinking, and of course the work of the Holy Spirit.

The challenge of moving beyond the m0 and m1 crowds is that because of the greater cultural distance, seeing the gospel take root is a longer, more difficult process. If we have m0 expectations for an m3 group, we'll be disappointed. Think about what Paul walked into at Mars Hill—polytheism on steroids, learned Epicurean and Stoic philosophers from seats of power and influence quickly dismissing him. Wildly divergent views of ethics and morality on everything from life and death to gender and sexuality. (Sound familiar?) Into this chaotic maelstrom, Paul preached "about Jesus and the resurrection" (Acts 17:18). He had further to travel in the world of ideas than he did with some of his other audiences. Given the cultural obstacles Paul faced at Mars Hill, seeing *anyone* convert is a wild success!

Like Paul, we have to take into account the degree of difficulty, the long-range process, and the scope and variety of people groups on our campuses. It takes time to become established in cultural contexts different from ours so we can speak incarnationally and with integrity from within them. As ministers embedded in a rapidly shifting cultural campus context here in North America, we have to remember that most people are *not* right on the doorstep of belief.

The cultural distance from the gospel of certain student groups on my campus led me two years ago to start The Sojourn Forum for "questioning faith and doubt." In the group, we've talked about a number of the most common apologetic, philosophical, and theological issues that are common in New Atheist and interfaith discussions. Everyone from Hitchens and Dawkins to Nietzsche and Kierkegaard to Plantinga and Keller have become our conversation partners. Each semester, multiple officers from the atheist-agnostic student association have attended. In fact, they're my most consistent attenders. We also started the Skeptics' Bible Study group, in which we look at specific verses and passages related to common objections to Christianity.

I have great relationships with many of these unbelieving students. I'm genuinely friends with a number of them. I have their ears in ways that very few other Christians—if any—do. And they've confided things to me, like Yasic's prayer request. Still, in two years, I haven't seen many coversions among that particular group of people from Sojourn. It's not the only thing I do, but it's an important part of my work. Is this a *failure*?

A while back, I received a Facebook message from a student I had met with the previous academic year but had lost track of since. Back then, he was a very heady and intellectual skeptic. He told me that he had become a Christian in the last couple months, and that my "Jesus group" had played a part in that. This wasn't a kid I had seen much of for a year, and I didn't get to lead him to faith in Christ. But God saw fit to take the seeds that had been planted and bring them to fruition—and I got to be part of the process.

Instant Fruit?

We often talk about the fruitfulness of the kingdom as if it can be generated instantly. It can't. It takes time, and it's mysterious—only God can make it grow. What appears to happen instantly has always been preceded by other means of God's work, including other people. If there are fewer means in our culture to influence people toward the gospel, then our work will begin at an earlier point in the process. While I would like to see more instant fruit from my work with non-Christians, I can look back at many other ways God has worked. We had meaningful conversations every week, the gospel was shared repeatedly, some big "defeaters" of the gospel were challenged and knocked down, real friendships were formed and deepened, and our network of relationships grew.

I've also seen an overflow effect from engaging with skeptics—an effect that is bearing fruit among the Christian students with whom I work. They have become more solid in their own beliefs and confident in their ability to share their faith. They've told me that seeing me engage the most vocal critics of Christianity on campus has emboldened them to share the gospel with their friends and classmates. I regularly talk and correspond with students who are asking, "How do I respond to my Muslim friend . . . my atheist friend . . . my Religious Studies professor . . . ?" When these things are happening, I can trust God for the future fruit.

It's tempting to chase the easier results we see when we engage culturally close students. I too have seen more "instant" conversions in reaching the m0 and m1 students. But we can't abandon our responsibility to push beyond these culturally close people groups. To begin to really reach our campuses, we must be willing to engage people's questions and objections. In an environment in which students are being taught to question and assess everything, being open to listening to them shows we care about them beyond simply wanting to convert them to Christianity.

Verbal witness, in all its various modes, is essential. Although it will rarely happen quickly, once people *are* willing and interested in having conversation about our faith, we need to know what to say. Evangelizing means that at some point, we have to verbalize our faith. Many good resources exist to help us do that, but the key is to not rely on pre-packaged spiels. While they can help train us and get us to a certain comfort level, like a script they are put to the side when it comes time to engage the audience. This generation, in particular, values authenticity. Sharing the gospel will always have content, but it must be in our own words, interwoven with our story and experiences, saturated with scripture, prefaced by prayer, and in dependence on the Holy Spirit.

Going "Down and Out"

So how do we engage each of our groups on the cultural distance continuum?

m0: For this group, a competent campus minister doesn't have to do much more than show up. If you build a fellowship group, this group (plus some of the m1s) are the first ones who will come. Ministry to this group of people is necessary and essential. Many ministries excel at training their staff and students to reach this group and possess more than enough quality resources to do so. But generally speaking, the other 80 to 90 percent of the student body are probably not coming to the large group meetings. Even worse, the m0 "share of the market" is rapidly shrinking. But it's a shame that the vast majority of campus ministry efforts, personnel, and resources are disproportionately spent here on this rather small slice of the pie. I'm not against investing in a small group of people, but our focus must be to disciple them in order for them to make disciples.

m1: This is usually who we're reaching through "friendship evangelism." Community is often a doorway here, so we must ask if we're incarnating a rich, vibrant community. Is it open or closed? Inward or outward facing? Hidden or visible to outsiders? Existing for its own ends or participating in larger, redemptive purposes?

On the campuses where I've served, m0s and m1s are those who are most easily gathered and most readily discipled. But as I've already mentioned, the problem is that these groups are shrinking. The future of college ministry is in what Alan Hirsch calls the "missional-incarnational impulse,"[5] going both *out* in mission and *down* in incarnational depth—or we could say "down and out." Our mission implies direction.

What do I mean by "down?" It means incarnating ourselves among people groups who are far from God—like Jesus did. Jesus came "down" from heaven and humbled himself to become a man. Being humble and resisting the tendency to cling to our "rights" and preferences are part of the downward mobility of the gospel. Incarnational ministry also has to have a depth to it. Surface attempts at being like people will be found out in a second. Incarnational ministry isn't true to its name unless it has a deep integrity and authenticity. The future of college ministry is in taking a long-range process view and becoming all things to all people, so that by all possible means, I might save some (see I Corinthians 9:22).

What do I mean by "out?" Going out means leaving our safety zones and going far and wide. It means not being content with reaching Jerusalem and Judea, but taking Christ's message to the Samaria and the ends of the earth on our campus, to those who are ideologically far from us. It means acknowledging that college students are not one people group but many and requires our making a commitment to reach as many groups as possible. For too long, we've spent most of our time inside the friendly confines of reaching m0s and m1s, even doing much of our evangelism "in our camp" and wondering why we aren't seeing more people come to Christ. But Jesus modeled "going outside the camp."

A Provocative Faith

You'll notice that in this chapter I haven't given you much in the way of techniques. Instead, I've told stories of how I've shared the gospel in my particular context. I've given you questions to ask. I can't tell you what to do exactly because that's what you need to come to by reading your Bible, praying, listening to the Holy Spirit, and discerning the culture and people groups to whom God has sent you.

In all our interactions, we should aim to be provocative in the best sense, "calling forth" a response. In I Peter 3:15, Peter says, "Always be prepared to give an answer to everyone who asks you to give the reason for the hope that you have." This often-quoted verse reminds us to always be ready to share the gospel. But implicit in Peter's statement is that Peter assumes that people will be asking us why we believe what we do. There should be something different, distinctive, and compelling about us, or more specifically, the hope that is in us. When was the last time someone asked you why you believe what you do? The best evangelism is a person who has been radically transformed by the gospel and is unashamed of his or her faith in Jesus Christ. The best evangelism naturally flows from the kind of faith, faithful lifestyle, and faith-filled community that calls forth a response.

Chapter 7

GOING OUTSIDE THE CAMP

And so Jesus also suffered outside the city gate to make the people holy through his own blood. Let us, then, go to him outside the camp, bearing the disgrace he bore. For here we do not have an enduring city, but we are looking for the city that is to come.

Hebrews 13:12-14

In October 2008, my brothers and I had the unforgettable experience of being at Game 4 of the World Series in Philadelphia. We're longtime Phillies fans, so we enjoyed watching them win big, 10-2. We heckled the Rays players all night long with boos and jeers. As any Philly sporting event should be, it was an intense and memorable experience. On my drive home the next morning, I stopped for a break along the Pennsylvania Turnpike. I saw two women wearing Tampa Bay Rays gear, so (of course) I had to give them a little good-natured ribbing. I found out that one of the women was the cousin of the Rays pitcher from the night before— who had *not* had a good game. As we talked, she told me she had been surprised at how difficult it had been to find tickets and a hotel and how intense the fans were. I just laughed and said, "Well, what do you expect? This is Philly, and it's the World Series!" I hope she's recovered from her experience. Her faulty expectations set her up for a rather unpleasant evening as a fan of the visiting team.

As much as I care about my Phillies, that's just baseball. In ministry, our stakes are much higher. But like the Rays fan in that particular instance, we need to adjust our expectations. We need to expect that we'll bear reproach for our faith in Jesus—especially being a part of university culture, where being a Christian feels more difficult than ever before. Christian students know, or often soon learn, that few of their peers think positively of their beliefs.

In this context, we must ask ourselves, How do we live faithfully and proclaim the gospel faithfully? How do we live with the reproach, rejection, even hostility the world might have for us? Faithfulness is found by going to Jesus outside the camp, by joining him outside the places of security and power, by voluntarily going to places that might not receive us well. Jesus is there, but going outside the camp isn't easy.

Going outside the camp means *loss*. Christ became powerless; he had no place to rest his head and did not cling to material things or comfort. He lost relationships and was despised and rejected, even by his own family. Going outside the camp also means *shame*. He was the victim of a sham trial, treated as a common criminal, and stripped and beaten. He was mocked and laughed at and abandoned in his moment of greatest need. He felt the reproach of those he created and came to save. Finally, going outside the camp means *keeping a greater goal in view.* Jesus, "for the joy set before him endured the cross, scorning its shame" (Hebrews 12:2), focusing not on the now, but on "the city that is to come." Jesus did all this for our salvation, our redemption. Of course, his saving work is unique. Though he was God, he emptied himself and did not cling to any of his divine privileges (see Philippians 2).

But in doing so, Jesus also demonstrated the way we must live and proclaim the gospel—not through power and riches, but in weakness and loss. Not through fame and the applause of the world, but often in shame. Not with comfort and ease in the here and now, but with our hearts focused on "the city that is to come." Going outside the camp means joining Jesus in laying down our lives so that others may hear the gospel. Just as Christ went "outside the camp" and bore reproach, so may we face mockery, loss of friendship, and loss of opportunity in order to faithfully proclaim Christ. The good news is that the gospel goes forward as we learn to embrace Christ's method of sharing the gospel in weakness. The good news is that the loss we feel will be used by God in redemptive ways. Even our apparent defeats—like Christ's—can become the scenes of kingdom victory.

The bad news is that many Christians in our culture and on our campuses have not embraced Christ's method. Instead of building bridges, they've sought to fight. Instead of coming in humility and weakness, they've sought power and been arrogant. I once read about a certain campus ministry that, when confronted with the normal red tape of trying to get established on a campus, played the First Amendment/religious discrimination card and *sued* the university. Yes, they eventually got on campus, but in the process they hurt their cause and damaged every other ministry already on campus whose leaders had been willing to go through the red tape. I'm not saying we should throw all legal rights out the window, but isn't it far better to embrace the God's-strength-in-our-weakness approach of the kingdom?

Reaching Those Outside the Camp

Going "outside the camp" brings us to the m2, m3, and m4 groups. They are the largest groups and the ones least reached by the gospel on our campuses because simply doing *more* of what we already do, trying *harder*, or doing the same things *better* will not reach them. These are different people groups who need to be reached differently. When we try the same approaches we always have, we're not that different from the missionaries of the colonial age who encouraged jungle natives to wear three-piece wool suits and drink tea because their narrow view of humanity and Christianity made them believe all Christians should look like they did.

Reaching M2s

I believe this group is the hardest group to engage, which might be surprising since this isn't the most hostile group. But that's exactly the problem. On the surface at least, they're completely apathetic. They're neither hot nor cold to the gospel. They don't want to talk about it, and the fact that you do probably makes them uncomfortable and offends them. So what can we do? Our mission is to push the needle toward more meaningful engagement and discussion. It seems that very few of our evangelistic strategies meaningfully engage this huge, absent majority. Ice cream socials, pizza parties, and root beer keggers may attract the m1s on your campus. High profile speakers and rigorous apologetics may engage the m3s and m4s. But what about this middle group?

Since they're not coming to us, how can we go to them? The challenge with m2s is that they're the only group not interested in talking. We can talk, but they aren't listening. That doesn't mean they don't have opinions about Christians and Christianity—they most certainly do. But they're often inconsistent and ill-informed opinions drawn from a hodgepodge of pop culture and personal experiences.

How do we speak to a group that isn't listening? Rather than speaking our foreign language over and over, we have to speak in a language they understand. This is where our nonverbal witness and example become very important. When we join God in his redemptive purposes, we do things for the good of our school, our community, and our world. These things, when done with sincerity, command attention and build bridges. When we look for ways to partner in the things they care about, we eventually win the right to be heard through the impact and integrity of our actions. The power of humility and service can open doors for our evangelism if we "live such good lives among the pagans that, though they accuse [us] of doing wrong, they may see [our] good deeds and glorify God on the day he visits us" (I Peter 2:12).

Reaching M3s and M4s

I remember sitting down for the first time with a particular student and asking her to tell me her story. Though she had not been raised in a very religious household, she became extremely interested in spiritual subjects as a teenager. For about a year, she attended youth group with a friend. At one point during this time, the youth pastor was talking about sexuality, about which she had big questions. When she voiced them, he accused her of trying to sidetrack and even sabotage the group and refused to answer her questions. Not long after, she stopped attending. When I met her a few years later, she was the president of the university's pagan society.

I wasn't there, so I don't know exactly what happened. Perhaps both parties could have behaved differently. But here's what I do know: for a solid year, a Christian youth group had a would-be pagan participating in their ministry, but no one bothered to engage her or her questions on a meaningful level, and when she tried to voice them, she was shot down. Is it any wonder she went another way and is more than a little suspicious of Christians?

Yet to her credit, I found this student to be a willing dialogue partner once I made it clear I felt comfortable being the "visiting team." We've had some great discussions between our groups. I've found that some of the pagans and even some of the self-described militant atheists on my campus are among the friendliest and most willing to dialogue. Surprising, huh? And while personal friendliness does not always correlate to openness to the gospel, we can make the most of relational opportunities in many ways, through everything from constructive conversations and bringing in speakers to neighborhood cleanups and even missions trips.

If you're a campus minister, what percentage of your ministry time, energy, and resources do you spend on m0s compared to everyone else? What percentage of the content that you deliver to m0s is intended to help *them* reach out to everyone else? Is it any wonder that ministries are an increasingly shrinking, irrelevant minority on our campuses today? What would it look like to overhaul the way we do ministry so that even the *majority* of what we do is designed to engage the other 80 to 90 percent of the campus who will never find their way to our fellowship meetings?

The gospel is not meant to culminate with us but to compel us outward (see 2 Corinthians 5). The living water of Christ is meant to flow in a river, not end in a stagnant swamp—and God's grace always wants to flow "outside the camp." As we keep our eyes on Christ and the city that is to come, we can face reproach, knowing God will use it for his good, lasting purposes. Engaging those outside the camp gives us a great opportunity to share the gospel in different, surprising, and even subversive ways. Here's what I mean.

1. Subverting by Thinking Differently

Engaging students will eventually lead to us having an initial conversation with each of them about our faith. But before starting these conversations, we should be thinking, Where is the conversation about Jesus already happening, and how can we join in? Jesus is the "stuff" of hundreds—maybe even thousands—of conversations on campus every day in classes, after class, in the dorms, over meals. Listening well helps us hear these conversations.

But before assuming we know who we are supposed to reach or that we will happen upon opportunities randomly, we must first ask ourselves and God, Who is not being reached, and what can I do to reach them? Before placing people in camps of "friend" and "enemy," I try to consider, who might this person be if Jesus got ahold of them? Paul makes it clear in 2 Corinthians 5:16 that we're not supposed to look at people "from a worldly point of view." We look at them through God's eyes.

When I arrived at Penn State, my stated desire was to reach "the other 43,000," that is, the students not already involved in one of the existing evangelical fellowship groups—the unchurched and dechurched. Forty-three thousand is a lofty goal though, to say the least, and setting this target helped me narrow things down only a little bit. While I was never an apologetics all-star and didn't have any particular reason to minister to skeptics except that they were there, ready to talk, we hit it off from the time my ministry began.

2. Subverting by Looking for Different Opportunities

Instead of the usual approach of flyers and pizza, I took a different approach to reaching out to skeptics. Borrowing InterVarsity's concept of "proxe stations," I posted common objections to Christianity on a board—objections such as "The Bible can't be trusted," "God would never allow suffering," and "Christians are intolerant bigots," and invited people to put a little sticker next to the statement that most resonated with them. This approach was so effective that initially quite a few students mistook me for an atheist. This exercise led to some great conversations. Because I was seen as credible and willing to engage the real questions people had, not only did I meet the leading atheists right away, but they were the first names on my e-mail list. They came to my first meeting and I came to theirs. It was the beginning of a wonderful working relationship.

Our campus has a spiritual center, which is a great facility for many things, but not for what I wanted to do. For the people I was seeking to reach, meeting in that physical space would have communicated that I was the home team. So instead of defaulting to the usual meeting spaces, I checked out the local indie café/used bookstore with the vegan menu and rainbow flag out front. I quickly identified this off-campus hangout in the downtown area as a place where unreached people gathered. I prayed for open doors (see Colossians 4:2-6) and after some time hanging out there, approached the owner about hosting a faith-and-doubt book club. She was more than willing: she was enthusiastic! "Oh, we haven't had a book club here in a while—that would be great!" She was a "person of peace," and she always made sure our discussion area was reserved and open for us. We met there every Thursday night for two years.

To be honest, this location did scare off some of the Christian students who felt uncomfortable venturing into an establishment like this one. They were the students who expected our meetings to affirm their tidy categories of good guy/bad guy, the students who wanted the Christians to smack down the atheists every week. At this gathering, the tone we set was different because it subverted the expectations of both non-Christian and Christian students.

3. Subverting by Treating Others Differently

There is a preacher at Penn State who is a university legend for all the wrong reasons. He stands outside one of the big classroom buildings all day and shouts fire and brimstone, and he's often heretical. For example, he claims to have killed over 600 people through the power of prayer. Atheists make it their personal mission to argue with him, and many of them often hang out there. His presence frames much of the debate and discussion about religion on campus.

Most Christians don't really know what to do or say about him, but everyone notices and remembers his pride, arrogance, condescension, and especially the ridiculous arguments and cases for Christianity he's made. There was even an incident between my atheist friends and this man in which the police were called. People said he threatened to pull a knife on the students. This incident was covered in the newspaper and found its way onto YouTube. While the whole event was blown out of proportion, it still confirmed the worst stereotypes: Christians are ridiculous, arrogant, ignorant, hypocritical, and even a little dangerous. This man is one of the main defeaters of the gospel on campus.

How can we share the gospel when this is the type of Christianity people are observing and to which they're reacting? We must show that *we* need the gospel. If we want to talk with those outside the camp, we have to give up the idea that our goal is to win the debate. Even if we could, trying to win is the wrong approach. No, it's with humility and in weakness that we must proceed. This is definitely outside our comfort zone, and we need the gospel in order to make this a reality—the gospel power of not having all the answers, of being willing to be shown when you're wrong, of showing you can take a punch and come back.

With my Sojourn group, there were plenty of times I didn't have all the answers, plenty of times I felt like I had failed them. And on a couple occasions, I've said things I later regretted. Yet these experiences have proved to be essential in building relationships. Not having all the answers shows I'm human. Needing to apologize shows I'm a sinner. Both point to my need for Jesus—and have allowed me to take the focus off me and our tangential arguments and on to him. Sharing the gospel in weakness is redemptive. This often means God redeeming our mistakes and even our sins against others. We should be close enough to unbelievers that we might sin against them. Close enough to them that they will care. Close enough that they see our need for Jesus.

One freshman communications major connected to my ministry wrote for the daily student newspaper. At one point, she did a story about the controversy surrounding the atheists having an office at the spiritual center on campus. The only problem was that there was no controversy! My atheist friends were justifiably angry, and so was the spiritual center. They complained, and the paper printed a retraction and suspended her. So she was out of a job—maybe a career?—and my atheist friends had one more complaint against the religious crazies.

I didn't know what to do. Both were my friends. I counseled the journalist to look for God's redemptive purpose in this situation. What if she were to ask them for forgiveness? So I organized a meeting between her and Dan—the president of the atheist group—and Yasic. I appreciated their willingness to meet and the trust they were putting in me. During the meeting, she apologized. She said (and I'm summarizing), "I made a mistake; please forgive me. I'm not perfect. This is why I need Jesus." Her apology improved the situation. It was the right thing to do, and it seemed to defuse their anger and outrage. Her willingness to apologize also turned a difficult situation into a redemptive one—an opportunity to share the gospel. Because she was willing to embrace loss, shame, and the hope of a greater future, she had the opportunity to share the gospel in her weakness.

People who are skeptical of Christianity can call us a lot of things. But if we go outside the camp and share the gospel in weakness, they shouldn't be able to call us arrogant or hypocritical. When we come in humility, we've accomplished something real. We've removed, or at least put a dent in, one of the main defeaters of belief.

Chapter 8
MAKING DISCIPLES WHO MAKE DISCIPLES

Christianity without discipleship is always
Christianity without Christ.[1]
—Dietrich Bonhoeffer

Several years ago, campus ministers at the University of Texas looked at their campus of over 50,000 and saw that only 6 percent of the campus population was meaningfully involved in Christian fellowship. This realization led several ministries, including Campus Renewal, Hill Country Bible Church—UT, and the college ministry of the Austin Stone Community Church, to make radical changes in how they ministered. No longer content to wait for students to come to them, they began intensively discipling their students to reach out to those in their relational networks. They placed their students in communities that targeted particular people groups, whether they were students in a dorm, on a team, in a club, or elsewhere. Today, these missional communities are snowballing and have had a transformative effect on the campus. In five years, these ministries estimate that the percentage of students actively involved in Christian fellowship has risen from 6 percent to 11 percent![2]

It's not that these ministries weren't discipling the students before, but their efforts weren't sufficiently leading to mission. The changes they made came about through making some very intentional, sometimes hard-fought decisions in how these ministries discipled their students. In some cases, they radically altered their entire ministries in order to disciple their students for the mission: they dethroned large group meetings as the supreme college ministry gathering, changed their traditional evangelistic techniques, and made sure they weren't reducing discipleship to absorbing Bible knowledge and asking accountability questions. Their focus became making disciples who would reach the campus, shifting from viewing discipleship as a program to making disciples who make disciples for the mission.

Hearing the Great Commission Again for the First Time

You've probably heard the Great Commission a thousand times. At least it seems that way, right? Chances are you've taught on it many times as well. The danger with passages like this is that they become so familiar that we forget how radical they are, and we become inoculated to a message we need to hear. So as you read it again, imagine you're standing with the bewildered disciples, hearing it for the first time. It must be important—otherwise Jesus wouldn't have made it his parting instruction:

All authority in heaven and on earth has been given to me. Therefore go and make disciples of all nations, baptizing them in the name of the Father and of the Son and of the Holy Spirit, and teaching them to obey everything I have commanded you. And surely I am with you always, to the very end of the age. (Matthew 28:18-20)

Jesus' message to his followers was to "make disciples." This is a huge, all-encompassing command. It is not merely one command among many, but the goal of many other commands. We evangelize, worship, teach, gather in community, and show mercy—but in doing all these things, we are to be *making disciples*. If we are not making lifelong disciples of Jesus, we are doing the wrong things or doing them in the wrong way. If we *are* making disciples, then what we do will last for eternity and result in greater glory to God.

As we see in the Great Commission, evangelism was never meant to be divorced from discipleship, and neither of these can be divorced from mission. Many ministries are discovering that making on-mission disciples is the best evangelistic strategy they can initiate. Still, making lifelong disciples is a challenge, a truth to which any of us who have wrestled with our students drifting away from the Church and Jesus after graduation can testify.

Therefore, we should be asking the question, How does this make disciples? If we're serious about ensuring we're on mission, we will evaluate every program, every meeting, every event, every dollar we spend, and even every staff position by asking how each one serves to make disciples. Some aspects of our ministry will be affirmed and bolstered, others will need to be tweaked, and some will need to be axed if they don't serve the goal of making disciples.

Why Is Making Disciples Such a Challenge?

Making disciples is a challenge for many reasons. The "tyranny of the urgent" is particularly strong in campus ministry, where life-shaping conversations, processes, and events are crammed into fifteen-week semesters. There is always a lot going on. In this context, if making disciples isn't built into the DNA of who we are, it will get shortchanged. Yes, we might talk about discipleship, but not everything we do contributes to it.

Campus ministry can't be concerned only with the programs, events, or activities that are happening next week. We must focus on the spiritual formation of students for the missio Dei, a lifetime of following Jesus and joining him in his mission, making our goal to *make disciples for the mission of God*. After all, wasn't that Jesus's primary goal?

Jesus proclaimed the good news that his hearers could join him in a new way of life. More than simply offering a message of personal salvation, Jesus invited his followers to participate in God's redemption of the world.[3]

Our approach to articulating a vision of discipleship ought to be based upon Jesus' own call to discipleship.

What *Is* a Disciple?

A disciple is a Christian, and a Christian is a disciple. As a result of our modern obsession with compartmentalizing, we have acted as if there are two kinds of people in the Church—Christians (the ones who "asked Jesus into their heart") and disciples (the ones who are more serious, more *disciplined* about their faith). But this isn't a biblical distinction. There is no such thing as a Christian who is not following Jesus. There is no allowance for someone to have Jesus as their Savior but not Jesus as their Lord. There is no such thing as a Christian who does nothing but sit around, passively absorbing content. The word "disciple" is used 230 times in the gospels and twenty-eight times in Acts. It is by far the most common way of referring to the people who followed Jesus and placed their faith in him.[4]

Being a disciple means following Christ. More than that, it means responding daily to Jesus's instruction that "if anyone would come after me, he must deny himself and take up his cross and follow me" (Mark 8:34). This is a comprehensive following: it means to follow him in everything, even unto death. As Dietrich Bonhoeffer said, "When Christ calls a man, he bids him come and die."[5] Where discipleship is involved, there is no room for a simple decision of faith divorced from genuine commitment and the rigors of following Jesus. Robert Webber tells us that the early church's process of discipleship was so rigorous that it could take *years* before an individual would be a full member of the community.[6]

To be a disciple is to obey *everything* Jesus taught us. It is not merely to give cognitive assent to a set of truths but to belong to a community. It is to be increasingly conformed, by grace, to Christ, and means joining him in his redemptive mission and heeding his sending and discipling commands, including Matthew 28:18-20 and John 20:21: "As the Father has sent me, I am sending you!" Similarly, the essence of discipling others is to say with Paul, "Follow me as I follow Christ." Being a disciple is always about Christ.

> The concept of discipleship Jesus introduced ran counter to the prevailing notion of the teacher-disciple relationship. Jesus was not making disciples who would learn of him, become independent of him, and then make disciples of their own. His goal was that his disciples would make disciples not of themselves but that they would go forth to make disciples of Jesus.[7]

The extent to which we enter the picture is only the extent to which we are conformed to Christ. This conformation must include following him in his redemptive mission.

"Do vs. Done" Discipleship[8]

Because we follow Jesus Christ, true discipleship is always centered on the liberating and radical grace extended to us through him. I can't overstate how crucial this is because our failure to keep discipleship gospel-centered is the very reason so many Christians find it distasteful. The gospel is about what Jesus has done to save us, not what we do to save ourselves. Gospel-centered discipleship is about living into our identity as accepted, adopted sons and daughters of God, and following Jesus by the strength and power he provides. The discipleship that many of us have experienced is often about self-control, self-reliance, self-righteousness when we "succeed" and self-reproach when we "fail." Gospel-centered discipleship is about celebrating and growing into our acceptance while works-centered discipleship is the ill-fated, soul-sucking, burnout-inducing attempt to earn God's approval.

The kind of discipleship that results in campus-saturating movements doesn't rely on people trying to prove to God, others, and themselves that they are worthy. Gospel-centered discipleship tells us we're *not* worthy, that we *can't* measure up, and it's only by grace that we'll become like Jesus. While works-centered disciples spend most of their time looking down on everyone else or themselves for not measuring up, gospel-centered disciples spend their time looking up in wonder at the grace they have been shown. While works-centered disciples are usually arrogant or depressed, gospel-centered disciples radiate joy and exude a holy confidence. While works-centered disciples are profoundly self-focused, morbidly introspective, and narcissistic, gospel-centered disciples are Christ-focused and radically others-focused. While works-centered disciples try to run on the fumes of self-effort, gospel-centered disciples are propelled by the grace and power of God. To follow Christ works the same as being saved by him—by grace, through faith.

Have you ever watched one of those home improvement shows? A few years ago, some friends of ours were on *Trading Spaces*. This was before the days of tear-jerking extreme home makeovers, so with the makeover team, they just performed some cosmetic changes that consisted of buying new pillows, adding a fresh coat of paint, and rearranging furniture. But despite their TV home "makeover," their home looked pretty much the same. It wasn't until years later, when they had a huge addition put on, that their home was transformed.

Works-centered discipleship—the kind for which we have such distaste, the kind in which the Pharisees and every legalist since them have indulged—makes cosmetic changes but fails to truly transform. It cleans things up a bit and makes for a good appearance, but nothing is really different. On the other hand, gospel-centered discipleship works from the inside out to truly transform someone. The emphasis is not on the external behaviors or the rigor with which we perform them. It's on receiving the grace of God, which alone can save and change us.

The Problem with Small Groups

"But wait," you might be saying. "We already work hard at making disciples. In fact, we have a number of small groups designed to do just that!" The problem is that many of our small groups are not doing all that we need them to. Jeffrey Arnold discusses the shortcomings of small groups in his book *Small Group Outreach*. He writes,

Spiritual hunger is at an all-time high, yet the church of Jesus Christ has not effectively mobilized its small groups to reach out beyond themselves and grow. While groups bond well and care deeply, they seem to encounter difficulty in growing and in caring for people beyond their group . . .

Yet the cultural impact of small groups has been relatively weak. The small group movement is succeeding less because it is bucking the system than because it is going with the flow. It does not offer a form of community that can be gained only at great social or personal cost. Instead, it provides a kind of social interaction that busy, rootless people can grasp without making significant adjustments in their lifestyles.

On the one hand, the small group movement has unbelievable potential; on the other hand, its impact is less than impressive. How can we reverse our natural preoccupation with ourselves and our needs? How can we touch the hearts of groups and their members to consider the plight of the unsaved? How can we motivate our people for service, outreach and justice?[9]

Does this description sound uncomfortably familiar? Let me suggest that the reason we fail to not only make *new* disciples, but hold on to the ones we have, is that our discipleship processes often lack essential missional foundations. This is particularly the case in what we could call Just Small Groups Syndrome, or JSGS.

JSGS emphasizes intellectual/cognitive knowledge instead of whole-life conformity to the truth. We've compartmentalized the learning from the being and doing. In the college ministry realm, we've implicitly told students that they can't "do" until they've learned enough. But Jesus taught his disciples through doing. What constitutes a successful small group? A team of people who would win Bible Jeopardy, or people who don't just hear the word, but do it? JSGS creates consumers instead of disciples. It creates people whose only expectation is to get fed, people who feel threatened if we call them to more than that. JSGS creates inward-facing, self-concerned communities instead of outward-engaging teams of missionaries.

What if discipleship weren't viewed apart from mission? What if one of the ways we grew in the gospel was not only through community but through being embedded in a community in which people are on mission together?

We need more than small groups. We need missional communities— teams of students who share a burden for a particular people group and come together for the shared purpose of reaching that group together. They come together in community to preach the gospel to each other and to help each other share it with others. They come together for prayer, encouragement, and equipping. They come together to model the kind of community into which they're inviting others. They're not a once-per-week meeting but a team or band committed to a common purpose.

The Parable of the Castle and the Campfire

How is this different from what you're already doing? Think of it in terms of this parable. Some people once found an incredibly precious, beautiful pearl. They gathered together and agreed that the countryside could be quite dangerous, what with all the ravenous beasts wandering around. They named themselves the People of the Pearl and started building walls to keep themselves—and their treasure—safe. Eventually, this building project became a full-blown castle complex, with everything they needed on the inside. The People of the Pearl became known as "insiders," a term they proudly embraced. While they didn't want to be exclusive, they didn't want to ruin the good thing they had going or lose their treasure, so their contact with "outsiders," as they came to be known, steadily diminished. Inside the castle walls, they also trained themselves in everything from waxing eloquent about the pearl to fighting to defend it.

Occasionally, an outsider would become curious about the castle. He would get close but often find the structure to be imposing, even frightening. The hierarchy that governed the lives of the insiders seemed strange to the uninitiated. Amazingly, even though the pearl was printed on nearly every sign and seal in and around the castle, the outsiders knew next to nothing about it! They had never even seen it. While the castle insiders came out to look around and even converse with the outsiders now and then, there was only one way to really connect with the insiders: you had to catch them during the one time every week when the drawbridge happened to be down. Outsiders were welcomed into the castle as long as they adopted the insiders' customs, language, and dress.

The exclusion of the outsiders didn't sit well with the castle insiders. So one brave person volunteered a suggestion: "Let's take our castle life on the road! We need to be in more than one place, and we need to be less intimidating to the outsiders. So here's what we'll do: let's build some small castles throughout the countryside, and stock them with things the outsiders like. Then it will be easier to invite outsiders to come in! We may even get to tell them about the pearl."

The castle insiders were excited by this idea, so they sent out groups. But their excitement quickly gave way to serious problems. It took a lot of work to prepare these groups to head out. Though they went to great pains to recreate all the elements of the castle within their little forts, people complained that their forts didn't have all the bells and whistles they wanted. Some wanted to go back to where they felt most comfortable. So they increased their trips back to the castle and reduced their hours in the forts. To top it all off, the outsiders were mystified by the small castles springing up in their countryside. The small castles didn't prove to be any more inviting, so the outsiders still weren't interested in coming in!

Despite these problems, the insiders had invested a lot of time, energy, and resources on the small castle plan, so they pledged to stick with it even though it hadn't really changed their relationships with the outsiders much. Then one of the small castle leaders had an epiphany. Without delay, he gathered up only his essential belongings and announced that he was leaving the fort. The other insiders looked at him with deep concern. Most of them assured him that they would *not* be leaving their small castle with him. They warned him he might lose access to the pearl if he left, that he would be vulnerable and defenseless. But a few joined him, and they exited their fort.

They then set up camp. They watched how some of the outsiders did things, and they adapted. It was difficult at first because they weren't used to life on the outside, but before long, they got a roaring campfire going, and some outsiders joined them for a meal. They found the outsiders to be much friendlier and engaging than they had previously assumed (not having talked with them much, they discovered they had many incorrect assumptions). The outsiders treated them differently outside the castle walls, too.

Soon, they found a particular tribe of outsiders with whom they clicked, and they combined camps. They continued their campfire meetings, and when they got the campfire going, and invited the outsiders to join them, they not only felt a deeper connection to the pearl, *but it was really there with them.* They had thought all along that you had to be *in* the castle to be near the pearl. But when they got out of the castle and built a campfire, there it was.

The campfire crew were amazed and thrilled with the life they had discovered. People in the small castles had become bored and suffered because they felt removed from the pearl. Some had assumed that going further out would make this worse. But the opposite proved to be true. Eventually many "insiders" lived on the outside, and many "outsiders" became "insiders." The terms became almost useless, so they just returned to calling themselves The People of the Pearl. The walls of the castle were knocked down, and the glory of the pearl rose to unimagined heights.

Chapter 9
DISCIPLING COMMUNITIES FOR THE MISSION

To become a disciple means a decisive and irrevocable turning to both God and neighbor.[1]

—David J. Bosch

As we've already addressed in previous chapters, many campus ministries exist as inward-facing insider clubs on campus where we disciple the insiders but never realize that the best discipleship happens when we go outside the camp. This is what missional communities help us do. The good folks of Hill Country Bible Church—UT, a church at the University of Texas in Austin (with a lot of student involvement), have built missional communities into the foundation of their ministry. They excel at coaching and mentoring their leaders. They also do a great job of keeping missional goals in front of their student leaders.

How do these student-led missional communities engage their people groups? Discipling people toward Christ is a process, and because we live in a post-Christian culture, we're often starting earlier in the process. We need to help students see how their missional discipleship is indeed a process. As a guide for this goal, I've adapted some of the language HCBC —UT uses to teach their missional communities of students and have included them here:

The Three "E's"

1. Explore

Identify who you're reaching. Who are they? What are they like? What do they value? Where do they gather? What do they do for fun? Get to know them. Make your first forays into their world, and befriend them. Discover what you have in common and what you don't. Make a few significant relational connections.

2. Engage

Having identified a few key individuals to whom you're seeking to especially reach out, you can become more intentional about connecting with them. You know the group, and they know you—hopefully they have even accepted you to a certain degree because you're a regular at the places and events they value. Over coffee or a meal, or during a run together, you seek to have spiritual conversations with them. These aren't full-fledged gospel presentations; rather, they are opportunities for you to feel out what they believe and chances for them to learn more about your beliefs and background. The beauty of spiritual conversations is that you can get to them from anywhere. Every day offers at least one news story from around the world or on campus that can raise spiritual questions.

3. Express

This is where you seek to have gospel conversations, expressing the truth as clearly as possible. Over time, as you have formed a relationship with each other, you've earned some credibility and trust. You both have an idea of how the other lives and why you believe what you do. You've demonstrated that you care about them rather than just about converting them.

Every non-Christian we know fits somewhere in this process. So as these missional communities gather together to talk and pray about their mission, they can ask who they're reaching and what the next step is. I like how HCBC-UT's mentors coach their students. They ask "What's the *win* this week?" This is a shorthand way of asking, "What's a reasonable goal for you this week? What would you consider a success?" The advantages of this approach are that they take mountain size goals and bring them down to achievable objectives.

By now, you might be asking, Aren't these steps for evangelism rather than discipleship? But we need to be discipled in order to evangelize, and genuine discipleship leads to mission. Discipleship includes learning—but we learn so we can equipped for mission. Discipleship includes accountability, but this includes being accountable for our mission. Discipleship means following, but this means following Jesus in his redemptive mission.

Mission is essential in our discipleship because it has this incredible way of bringing to the surface the very things that keep us from following Jesus. We can connect our discipleship to gospel, community, and mission by asking questions like:

- What is the gospel? How do you explain it to yourself and others? How are you doing that currently?
- How are you loving God (that is, cultivating communion with God, through all-of-life worship and spiritual disciplines)? How have you

grown in this area over the past week (or two weeks, or month)? How will you grow in this area over the coming week?

- How are you fulfilling the commands to love one another? Do you have any grudges or unresolved conflicts? Are you gathering and growing in a gospel-centered community with other believers? How have you grown in these areas over the past week (or two weeks, or month)? How will you grow in these areas over the coming week?

- How are you loving your neighbors? Are you living all of life on mission, through serving and engaging people where they are now? Where are you exploring, engaging, and expressing? How have you grown in these areas over the past week (or two weeks, or month)? How will you grow in these areas over the coming week?

Mission is an amazing crucible for discipleship for a number of reasons. It forces us to prioritize our time and to make hard choices, to deal with our temptations and to articulate why we believe what we believe. It confronts us with our idols and forces us to deal with our sin and its consequences. Because engaging in real ministry with real people brings real issues to the surface, mission forces us to read our Bibles, to really pray, and to deal with responses like "I don't want to" and "I don't like that person." And because we'll never make it alone, mission forces us to join together in community.

Why Mission Flows from Community

I. Jesus modeled it with the first disciples.

Even Jesus didn't go it alone! Instead, he called disciples to himself to follow him and to join him in his mission (see Luke 6:13-17; Mark 3:13-19). In his book *The Master Plan of Evangelism*, Robert Coleman writes,

It all started by Jesus calling a few men to follow him. This revealed immediately the direction his evangelistic strategy would take. His concern was not with programs to reach the multitudes, but with men whom the multitudes would follow. Remarkable as it may seem, Jesus started to gather these men before he ever organized an evangelistic campaign or even preached a sermon in public. Men were to be his method of winning the world to God.[2]

As we read the story of how Jesus makes disciples in the gospels and then births the Church in Acts, we see that gospel-shaped community leads to mission. Take for example the sequence in Luke.

In Luke chapter five, Jesus calls the first disciples while at the same time demonstrating the reality of the kingdom through performing miraculous acts. In chapter six, he clarifies the calling by narrowing down to the twelve disciples. This is gospel proclamation. In chapters seven and eight, Jesus is intent on teaching and equipping his community of disciples. All the while, the miracles he performs continue to testify to the new kingdom he has brought. This is community formation.

In Luke chapter nine, Jesus sends out the twelve on their first "mission trip." He commissions the disciples to go out on mission trips in community (Mark 6:7). This is missional sending. Significantly, this is *before* many of them even have a solid idea of who Jesus is! Peter's confession about Christ doesn't occur until later in chapter nine. In Mark's account, the sending of the twelve happens early in chapter six. This is before the feeding of the 5,000 and Jesus walking on water. After Jesus comes aboard the boat, Mark says, "They were completely amazed, for they had not understood about the loaves; their hearts were hardened" (Mark 6:51-52). Yes, you read that right. They were sent out on their first mission trip while their hearts were hard! It seems that part of Jesus' intention in sending them out is to evangelize them! Kingdom work begins early and often in Jesus' new community.

2. Paul and the early Church modeled it.

In Acts three and four, for example, we see that Peter and John continue the pattern of doing mission in community, which becomes the pattern of the early Church. We read in Acts 2:42-47 that the believers

> devoted themselves to the apostles' teaching and to the fellowship, to the breaking of bread and to prayer. Everyone was filled with awe, and many wonders and miraculous signs were done by the apostles. All the believers were together and had everything in common. Sell-

ing their possessions and goods, they gave to anyone as he had need. Every day they continued to meet together in the temple courts. They broke bread in their homes and ate together with glad and sincere hearts, praising God and enjoying the favor of all the people. And the Lord added to their number daily those who were being saved.

In the same way, when Paul said, "Follow me as I follow Christ," people followed! He was constantly surrounded by other people and plainly spoke of his need for them. Barnabas, Silas, Timothy, Luke, Sosthenes, Epaphras, Titus, and many more traveled with him. In nearly every epistle, he mentions his traveling companions, as well as his many friends. When his fellowship with Barnabas is broken, it's noteworthy because it's the exception to the rule.

Keeping Mission Prominent in Your Discipling Community

Does your group succeed because it does *not* ruffle feathers? Does it exist for busy, rootless people who don't like making adjustments to their lifestyles? Here are some of the things we've done, with varying degrees of success, to ensure mission is part of our foundational identity:

1. Decentralizing our ministry so missional communities become the primary form of ministry
2. Eating meals together every week to emphasize that our meeting is not just a Bible study but a place and time to connect
3. Meeting not in a "spiritual" place but in everyday places like dorm rooms, homes, lounges, apartments, coffee shops, bookstores, and so on
4. Regularly having outward-facing events (like brunches and parties) and service opportunities
5. Building mission into our discussion, application, and prayer every week
6. Regularly (weekly) stating our purpose as a group, and reviewing how we're doing every few months
7. Always encouraging those in to the group to invite others and to go to others

8. Encouraging spin-off initiatives, like my life group's "God on Tap," a monthly hangout for guys to talk Bible and life at our favorite sports pub

9. Making sure people are being shepherded by being proactive in talking with, and, when necessary, challenging those whose attendance and participation are suffering

10. Encouraging and empowering people to contribute what they have to offer, from food and childcare, to administration, to participation in our "worship potluck" nights, where we shelve our regular study and everyone contributes a song, scripture, or word of encouragement

The Fruit of Missional Discipleship

Ever wonder why some people fall through the cracks? Why they show up at large group meetings for a while then fade away? Even if we generally do a good job of communicating our purpose as ministries, we may still fail to translate that purpose into any clear plan or process for discipleship. Creating a plan will help cure us of several pathologies and move us into a new realm of kingdom fruitfulness.

1. Instead of confusion, clarity

We want people to understand and contribute to our vision and mission, but when we don't disciple them, they become confused about what they should do and how they can get there. They fill in the blanks themselves and expect things from our small groups and large groups that we can't (or shouldn't) give. Or they become content to merely attend, while filling the rest of their time with non-kingdom priorities. The students we serve aren't the only ones who are confused. Without a plan, ministry staff can lose focus, failing to understand why we do some things but not others. Without a plan, we are constantly busy but lack purpose and direction in what we do.

A discipleship plan should lead us to evaluate everything we do and should result in us bolstering some things and eliminating others. The plan should be *clear*. It should be simple, easy to explain, easy to remember, and easy to illustrate. Following Jesus should be simple, but not simplistic. It should be demanding, but possible for anyone. It costs us everything, but the yoke is easy and the burden is light.

2. Instead of paralysis, movement

Without a plan for discipleship, forward movement stops or occurs in fits and starts. Spiritual growth is stifled. People remain in immature states too long. Both new and old believers fall away. Those who are committed lack the necessary foundation for their service and, predictably, burn out.

But with a plan, people know what's next. They know where to jump in. Individuals have a goal and see the steps needed to get there. Too often, people in our ministries don't see anything compelling to do. It's only a matter of time before they check out. But discipleship that incorporates mission from the get-go never lacks movement at both individual and community levels.

3. Instead of sterility, reproduction

If we take discipleship out of the equation, we don't have a movement because we're not reproducing anything! Movements that don't disciple anyone don't create new disciples and hasten their own demise. Sterility means that we may be awfully busy, but we are not creating any new life.

But discipling for mission ensures that new life will be created from all our activity. As Jesus said, "Unless a kernel of wheat falls to the ground and dies, it remains only a single seed. But if it dies, it produces many seeds" (John 12:24). To truly become a disciple, we must die to ourselves. Pride, reputation, and ambition must be cut off and pruned. Otherwise, the mission—and our discipleship—will be stifled. But when we submit our lives and become willing to lose control, we'll see Jesus unleash the exponential power of his kingdom. When discipleship is happening, not only do we reproduce; we'll have something worth reproducing.

4. Instead of subluxation, alignment

Subluxation is the chiropractic term for partially dislocated, unaligned vertebrae. The more moving parts we have in our ministries, the easier it is for us to fall out of alignment. Even if we are not very programmatic, we discover how easy it is to jump to the latest trend, event, or pet project. We may find that we lack the mechanisms to bring our efforts into alignment. Thus we feel that we're pushing really hard, but because we're sometimes pushing against each other and not in the same direction, we're not really getting anywhere.

A comprehensive discipleship plan leads to everyone pulling in the same direction. When we are aligned around a common goal, people are united in raising the problem of mission, answering it with the gospel, and doing so in community.

5. Instead of following idols, following Jesus

The question really isn't, "Are you a disciple?" It's *"Who* are you a disciple of?" Everyone is a disciple; it's a question of whether you're following Christ or someone or something else. In certain cases, people may follow another *person* instead of Christ. This could be a boyfriend or girlfriend. It could be a successful figure they aspire to be like. But more likely, their idol, and the thing by which they are being discipled, is something like money, pleasure, power, or achievement. These cultural idols run rampant on our campuses. They are promoted in the classroom, in the party scene, and sometimes even in our ministries. True discipleship does battle with our idols and dethrones them so Christ takes his rightful place in our hearts.

The Priority of Discipling Communities-on-Mission

Many small groups succeed only because they cater to rootless people who squeeze their faith into a couple hours one night a week. But this is not the kind of community-on-mission to which true discipleship calls students. There should be ways in which what we're doing is inconvenient, difficult, and countercultural. We should help students resist the impulse to squeeze their discipleship in among a number of other extracurricular activities. We need to help them fight compartmentalization and fragmentation, where they serve and socialize in spheres that never intersect or overlap.

If we champion discipleship for the mission, we can reach our campuses in ways we never imagined. We'll be challenged but pleasantly surprised, and as we disciple students who make other disciples, we'll see our campuses saturated with gospel-shaped communities.

Chapter 10

NINE ROLES OF A MISSIONAL CAMPUS LEADER

The students of this generation want us

to be who we are.

College ministry is not one job—it's (at least!) nine. You'll need to play a number of roles. Like most people in ministry, we have to be generalists rather than specialists. While no one excels in all the areas we'll explore, college ministry needs leaders who are at least competent in all of them and are constantly seeking ways to improve their ministry.

1. Gospel Communicator

Because the gospel is the foundation of our faith, it is essential that we're able to communicate its message effectively to both Christians and non-Christians. Whether in a one-on-one or large group setting, whether we are gifted speakers or always find ourselves stumbling over our words, we should be teaching and explaining the gospel to others in everything we say and do. While evangelizing, or communicating the gospel to someone who doesn't yet believe, is an integral part of gospel communication, many of us find it exceedingly difficult to be ambassadors for Jesus in our postmodern world. An increasing population of people find evangelism offensive, awkward, inappropriate, and politically incorrect; at some universities, evangelizing is even a violation of campus speech codes.

But a case has been made for ambassador evangelism by a surprising source—magician Penn Jillette (of Penn and Teller), an avowed atheist. Perhaps you've seen his TV show *Bull$%&*￼* or watched his video clips on YouTube. In many of them, he makes fun of Christians and Christianity, and like everything else he does, he's very outspoken and bombastic. But a few years ago, he posted a YouTube clip about being given a Bible by a businessman who went to one of his shows in Las Vegas and stayed after to meet him. Penn describes the man in surprising terms: he calls him sincere, kind, and sane, even as the man transparently told Penn, "I'm proselytizing." He says the man looked him in the eye and wasn't defensive even though he most likely knew Penn is an atheist. Penn goes on to say,

> I don't respect people who don't proselytize. I don't respect that at all. If you believe that there's a heaven and hell and people could be going to hell or not getting eternal life, or whatever, and you think, "Well it's not really worth telling them this because it would make it

socially awkward" . . . How much do you have to hate somebody to not proselytize? How much do you have to hate somebody to believe that everlasting life is possible and not tell them that?[1]

And Penn isn't the only non-Christian who feels this way; I know many unbelievers who do not respect people who hide their convictions. They don't like charlatans and hypocrites. *They* know the importance of our message and that if we really believe it, we should be sharing it with others. Sharing the gospel is the only way to live with integrity: even the most militant opponents to our message are pointing that out. We shouldn't need atheists to tell us to evangelize!

2. Student

If we're to be effective college ministers, we have to be willing to be students again. I don't necessarily mean enrolling in classes for credit although that isn't a bad idea. I'm talking about making a commitment to ongoing learning. We are working in the field of education, after all, and the people we're working with are students. If we want to be respected and taken seriously by the people group to whom we're ministering, we must have many interests. We must be widely read on a number of subjects and experts on a few subjects—including the field of study in which we hold our undergraduate degrees. I've also found it beneficial to have some basic knowledge, and a willingness to learn more, on the more popular majors at my school. We don't have to be knowledgeable enough that we could replace their professors, but students are smart; they'll quickly discount us as authorities (or equals) if we can't keep up with them in at least a few arenas.

Our culture is constantly changing, which means it's imperative that whatever we studied in college, we must be students in our professional field as well. We will not be effective if we're not staying current on pop culture, theological views with which we identify as well as those we don't, and ways we can engage our audience. If you're reading this, you're already making strides in this area, but as a group, we campus ministers typically aren't very good students. We need more campus ministers who are willing to be lifelong learners: the health, sustainability, and effectiveness of our ministries depend on it.

3. Theologian

Everyone is a theologian in the sense that everyone has thoughts, beliefs, and opinions about God. We all have a functional theology that shapes our day-to-day life and ministry. Students are working out their own theology as well—though they may be barely conscious of that fact. In many cases, they're examining it for the first time, which means we have to be ready for every question from "Who made God?" to "Why should I trust the Bible?" to "Was the Reformation really the outworking of the conflict between Augustine's soteriology and his ecclesiology?" (Honestly, I've been asked this question.) We have the unique opportunity and responsibility to take a proactive role in grounding students in essential Christian doctrines of salvation, the trinity (Christology in particular), the Bible, the Church, and missiology. In order to do that though, we must be knowledgeable in these areas and know where to find answers for what we don't know.

One of the joys of campus ministry is its immediacy. Many of us train for our positions in a matter of weeks and hit the campus. We then plan and run around like mad for fifteen weeks, see some immediate and huge life changes among our students, and do it all again in the spring. Pretty soon, those students have moved on, and we start over with a new batch of students. But immediacy has its downside. In moving as fast as the wind, we risk becoming groundless, lacking sufficient rationale, understanding, and foundation for what we do. Since we're often reacting to who or what is right in front of us, we can be led to grab on to what is the newest, latest, and freshest. We rarely stop to consider, from a rigorous theological perspective, what it is we're doing.

We must be grounded in theological foundations in order to be effective and fruitful in the long term. Being knowledgeable in the areas of practical theology, biblical theology, systematic theology, and church history equips us to answer students' questions, serve as mentors who base our leadership on what the Bible has to say about living out our faith, and understand the context of the history that has led us and the Church to where we are right now. It will prepare us to do the long, hard work of going deep with students rather than settling for crowds that are as fleeting as spring flowers.

So Should We All Go to Seminary?

I don't think we should mandate that everyone in campus ministry go to seminary; I've met many campus ministers who have studied hard to become good campus theologians and didn't need letters after their name or time in a classroom to do so. But this isn't always the case; while self-teaching is sometimes an adequate education, many of us tend to study subjects and read books that support the views toward which we already sway. As a result, our knowledge becomes unbalanced—heavy in a few chosen areas and practically non-existent in other areas that really matter. The words, the thoughts, the *theology* that come about can sometimes make us cringe.

I speak as someone who is seminary-educated, as someone who is ordained in my denomination. I've worked for both a parachurch organization and a local church. For the sake of effective ministry and credibility in our context, it's advisable that each campus have at least one trained staff member who can speak intelligibly and credibly into things like higher criticism, typical philosophical questions, and so on. And in our culture, seminary generally serves as the avenue to get a grasp on these and other concepts.

4. Shepherd

College ministry is highly relational; this aspect of college ministry (or any ministry, for that matter) often proves to be one of the most difficult ones for introverts. But we all have relational strengths: whether we're better in one-on-one settings or in front of a large group, we simply need to be good with people *somehow* and learn and grow from there. Are you a good listener? Do you like meeting new people? Do you get easily irritated when people share their problems? Do you build and maintain healthy relationships with both sexes? Are you relationally mature, or do you find it difficult to move beyond surface conversations about television or which teams look good for the play-offs?

I have found that students are open to conversations more than church congregations, which means the relationships we build will in fact be the bridges for people to see and hear Jesus. Campus ministers must love people—love them in all their energy, vitality, and creativity. Love them in their immaturity, off-color jokes (I work mostly with guys), and sloppy time management. Love them through their eating disorders, their parents' divorces, and their crises of faith. Just love them. You may be the only person consistently in their life who really does!

Joe Paterno has recorded the most wins of any college football coach of all time; he's also a man of deeply held convictions. From the beginning of his tenure at Penn State, he has sought to cultivate not just football players, but men. He's made it clear that Penn State Football will do things the right way, will strive for "success with honor." In a profile in *Sports Illustrated,* Paterno offered some advice to his son Jay, who is an assistant coach. It's also a good piece of advice for campus ministers:

> Every player we have, someone—maybe a parent, a grandparent, someone—poured their life and soul into that young man. They are handing that young man off to us. They are giving us their treasure, and it's our job to make sure we give them back that young man intact and ready to face the world.[2]

In campus ministry, relationships are paramount. You may have gathered that I'm very much a vision/mission/strategy guy, so reminders like this one that I'm being entrusted with someone's *treasure* are helpful. It's an important perspective to maintain. I value interaction with parents because, while the kids may try to treat our interactions as coolly and casually as possible, I know many prayers have gone ahead of our meetings.

5. Counselor

You will also be a counselor. Generally we reserve that term for individuals who have Psychology or Counseling degrees—people who get paid to sit in a room with people and talk out their problems. While we shouldn't endeavor to replace them, some people still attach a stigma to professional counseling. For the students who do have serious issues to deal with—sexual or physical abuse, alcohol or drug dependence, divorce, and so on—it's often easier to talk to someone they trust rather than a stranger. Being in college ministry means you're signing up to take on other people's problems.

Of course, we don't counsel only distressed students who are dealing with intense problems and situations; more often, we help students talk through the classic college student issues—their relationships with parents, roommates, friends, and boyfriends and girlfriends. The death of their childhood dream as they change their major. The disappointment over a grade, a class, a job. We have the opportunity to counsel students, offering them loving support and possibly a unique perspective on how to deal with the stresses that accompany life at this sometimes hard to navigate time in their lives.

6. Coach

Because we have a title or some positional authority, people look to us for leadership. To lead, we need to be people who can juggle a number of priorities at once while not losing sight of our goals as a ministry and as Christians. And we need to do this in a way that distributes authority and responsibility, empowering the other leaders, whether full-time employees or volunteers, whether adults or students, with whom we minister.

As a college minister, one of our jobs is to equip our students to be as fruitful as they can be. To put *them* in the position to succeed. Our job is to do what only we can do and help them do what only they can do. If we're always the stars of the show and the ones receiving the accolades, perhaps we need to reevaluate and refocus our role on campus.

In my ministry, I seek every year to eventually hand off to students any Bible studies or discussion groups I lead. While I start the groups, I also disciple leaders to one day take the reins. To maintain constant leadership over the groups would be to shortchange their discipleship and create an unhealthy sense of dependency on me. While the transition to student leadership can often have a "sink or swim" feel to it initially, I have inevitably seen the most growth among those students who have transitioned to this form of leadership.

7. Mentor

Should college ministers and students be "buddies?" How should you relate to the students you lead? In his book *Youth Ministry 3.0,* Mark Oestreicher talks about lessons he's learned in how to relate to the youth he serves:

Early on in youth ministry, one of my biggest misconceptions was that it was my role to be a buddy to teenagers. My faulty logic told me that if I succeeded in becoming one of them—a peer—then I'd have access to influence their lives to a greater degree. It wasn't until I discovered that I'd accomplished this that I saw the folly of my thinking. I'd forfeited my place as a mentor in order to become a pal.

Missionaries don't pretend to be one and the same as the people they're living with and ministering to. How fake and offensive would that be? Instead, they humbly and cautiously engage with people, being ever thoughtful and caring about cultural context, while acknowledging their own visitor status. Even the great missionary stories of the last century in which the missionaries reached a beautiful place of being an accepted part of a tribal culture still bore this reality: No matter how much the tribe loved, appreciated, and accepted them, they were still the alien who was "other." . . .[3]

I think Oestreicher's words here apply to college ministry as well. I'll confess that I've wasted time and energy trying to be a friend to my students. I'm getting better at not falling into that self-limiting role, but after several years of college ministry, I still have to consciously work against my natural tendency to become a friend rather than an authority to my students—especially after I've known them a year or so. While there are certainly cases in which we can be students' friends and not lose our place as authority and mentor, most of our students have more than enough friends. We aren't called to be their friends. We're called to answer their questions, to help shape (or form for the first time) their theology and their faith. We're called to mentor and coach, to shepherd and communicate the gospel. Our calling is unique—it doesn't fit neatly into the clear, classic categories of peer/professor/parent. Of these three options, we usually choose peer, but the pull we feel to be their friend will render us the same as everyone else, and consequently will blunt our ability to share the gospel as someone they respect.

Many of us in ministry are people persons who want to be liked and accepted, but I've found it hurts the relationship: students don't *really* want me to be my buddy. They want me to be their friend, but the older, wiser, *honest* friend who can teach, guide, and help them make sense of things biblically. When I started out in college ministry, it was certainly easier to be their friend. In some ways, it was probably appropriate: I was only five years older than my seniors, and much of our humor and cultural reference points were the same. But now I'm sixteen years older than my freshmen, and that number is only going to increase. While I still have much in common with students, it would be absurd and pathetic for me to pretend we're the same. They would see right through me. The students of this generation want us to be who we are.

8. Entrepreneur

The constant turnover in college ministry means our field is fluid, dynamic, and fast-paced; as a result, those of us who work in the field must be self-motivated, self-disciplined, and self-starters. People who prefer to wait for instructions all the time will not thrive. Neither will those who prefer working within a neat, tidy structure. Our ministries will better flourish when we act as entrepreneurs in a sense—when we're energized by trying new ways to reach and engage students. When we are driven and motivated to identify problems and challenges then set out to over-come them, we take active positions in our ministry.

Increasingly, one of the most important questions we can ask is, Can you handle the freedom? In older forms of college ministry, new or in-experienced campus ministers could be given clear sets of instructions with parameters and benchmarks. Do this. Do that. Produce this result X amount of times. But newer forms of ministry demand increasing creativ-ity and entrepreneurship. They demand giving the campus minister the latitude to try new things, including the freedom to try things that aren't easily measured. The problem is that not everyone can handle the free-dom. In his book *Linchpin*, Seth Godin has this to say about freedom:

> The freedom of the new kind of work (which most of us do, most of the time) is that the tasks are vague and difficult to measure. We can waste an hour surfing the 'Net because no one knows if surfing the 'Net is going to help us make progress or connections. This freedom is great, because it means no one is looking over your shoulder; no one is using a stopwatch on you . . . Freedom like this makes it easy to hide, easy to find excuses, easy to do very little.[4]

Because every semester we're meeting new students and seeing oth-ers leave, whether because they've graduated, left the university for other reasons, or simply stopped coming to our times together, we have to allow our leaders, staff, and volunteers to engage the students who are there in new, effective ways. In this kind of environment, we need to sur-round ourselves with supportive people who have proven they can handle the freedom proactively and responsibly. They must be self-disciplined, dedicated people of good character. Only then can we afford them the freedom to play to their individual strengths in order to reach and engage students on our campuses.

9. Support Raiser

For many of us, raising financial support to provide for our material needs is a reality. Whether we have to raise our entire budget or just a portion, it's a skill set we have to wrap our heads around. Raising support challenges our courage and boldness as we're forced to ask people to get behind our ministries. It challenges our communication skills as we learn to effectively share our vision through speaking and writing and following up with those to whom we speak. It challenges our organizational and leadership abilities as we strive to keep a ministry going now while at the same time we attempt to keep it alive in the future. It challenges our faith as we learn to pray "Give us this day our daily bread" with new fervency.

Even if you don't have to raise support for your own salary, you will likely need or want to raise funds for ministry projects, missions trips, disaster relief, and so on. The art of building a network of financial partners who support your ministry is one of the best moves you can make for long-term sustainability and health.

Final Thoughts

My goal in delving into all these roles is not to discourage people from considering college ministry as a vocation but to encourage people to think of themselves honestly. While I don't know anyone, including me, who excels in all these areas, we who are in process serve and love a God who is committed to our growth and sanctification. As we develop in faith, reliance on Christ, character, and ministry skills, and do so by the grace God provides, we will bear fruit that will last.

Part Three

FRUIT THAT WILL LAST
MOVEMENTS WITH ETERNAL IMPACT

Chapter 11

MEANINGFUL PARTNERSHIP AS A CAMPUS-SATURATING STRATEGY

Christianity, which is based on the radically accepting grace of God for sinners, has become categorized as narrow, exclusive, intolerant, and disrespectful.

My two sons love playing together in the large sandbox we have in our backyard. They bring their shovels, pails, trucks, and other toys into the sandbox and have a blast with each other for hours—until they end up fighting over the same tiny square of sand. They can have tons of available space, more toys than they can use, and a beautiful afternoon, but somehow it seems a fight tends to punctuate the end of their time in the sandbox.

On many of our campuses, we're not unlike kids competing for a small square of the sandbox; we squander our funding, staffing, training, and resources because we're fighting for the same patch of the campus population and who gets to build their castle there—all while the other 90 percent of the sandbox remains untouched. As a result, it seems unity on our campuses is pushed aside. While many of us have friendly, dare I say *collegial*, relationships with other ministries and campus ministers, we don't go much beyond that. We know how to get along when we're supposed to, make polite small talk, and ask each other thinly-veiled questions to discern how big or healthy someone else's ministry is: at the same time, we are positively spinning our own. As a field, it's hard to shake the sense that college ministry is plagued by disunity at the important, meaningful, functional levels of ministry. In large part, we're not getting along when it comes to actually ministering.

Our warm relationships are tenuous unless we've logged a lot of time outside the walls of our particular organization or church and built up inter-ministry trust. Often, all it takes is the defection of one or two key students to a "rival" ministry to sour our relationships. The reasons for our disunity generally aren't trivial or petty things—they go down to the core of our mission. We feel that we *need* that opportunity, meeting space, or student, so it feels right to cling to those things when they are threatened or taken. But the rest of the campus (and world) is watching, and they're not amused. As far as they're concerned, our bickering is one more way we're ruining a perfectly nice day in the sandbox: they figured out a long time ago that it's a lot more pleasant when we all get along.

The Culture Gets It—and We Don't

A generation that preaches tolerance, mutual respect, and acceptance has contributed to the high water mark for inclusivism in our society. In the process, Christianity, which is based on the radically accepting grace of God for sinners, has become categorized as narrow, exclusive, intolerant, and disrespectful. Our missional contexts are "*uni*versities," but they are that in name only; they are actually inclusive "pluralversities." There is no unifying theory or unifying endeavor except the commitment to include (almost) everyone in a pluralistic environment of diverse, fragmented ideas, worldviews, and lifestyles. Obviously, Christians can be one of the groups looked at with suspicion as potential threats to this inclusive environment.

The watching world doesn't understand why Christians can't get our act together. "Shouldn't religion be about love and acceptance?" they wonder. Even pop culture gets it: the TV show *LOST* built much of its plot around the phrase "Live together, die alone." The miniseries *Band of Brothers* used the tagline, "They depended on each other. And the world depended on them." One recurring feature of many college movie plotlines is how a renegade group of misfits and outcasts unite to overcome a common foe. Campus culture is all about inclusivity. So is pop culture.

The dissonance we feel between the dominant "culture of acceptance" and Christian culture has become a major apologetics issue. It's a major objection to the faith voiced by non-Christians. One line of questioning I hear a lot is, Why are there so many churches, denominations, and ministries? How do you know yours is the "right" one within Christianity, let alone Christianity being the right religion among all other faiths? This is just one of many reasons why we need to address our unity problem.

The Unity Idol

Of course, the culture doesn't fully understand unity—not the biblical version of unity, that is. (But then again, neither do we!) The value of inclusivity has become one of our dominant cultural idols. It has been enshrined among the pantheon of other cultural idols, alongside things like personal autonomy. As a quasi-religion, it is worshiped, and its values are rigorously enforced: those in our culture who do not show the required levels of acceptance are taken to the media woodshed. The version of unity celebrated at the popular level is a twisted, distorted version of the real thing. It's one reason people stumble all over themselves to affirm every aberrant or unbiblical lifestyle choice. In this environment, it's essential that our campus ministries demonstrate that 1) We care a *great deal* about unity; 2) Christianity has been a radically unifying faith from its inception; and 3) Christian unity differs in several important ways from the pop culture version.

The Bible Cares About Unity

Scripture talks a great deal about unity. When Jesus prays for all believers in John 17, he prays, "May they be brought to complete unity to let the world know that you sent me and have loved them even as you have loved me" (verse 23). References to unity can be found all throughout the New Testament. I've included just a few verses below.

"Let us therefore make every effort to do what leads to peace and to mutual edification" (Romans 14:19).

"May the God who gives endurance and encouragement give you a spirit of unity among yourselves as you follow Christ Jesus, so that with one heart and mouth you may glorify the God and Father of our Lord Jesus Christ. Accept one another, then, just as Christ accepted you, in order to bring praise to God" (Romans 15:5-7).

"I appeal to you, brothers, in the name of our Lord Jesus Christ, that all of you agree with one another so that there may be no divisions among you and that you may be perfectly united in mind and thought" (1 Corinthians 1:10).

"There is neither Jew nor Greek, slave nor free, male nor female, for you are all one in Christ Jesus. If you belong to Christ, then you are Abraham's seed, and heirs according to the promise" (Galatians 3:28-29).

"As a prisoner for the Lord, then, I urge you to live a life worthy of the calling you have received. Be completely humble and gentle; be patient, bearing with one another in love. Make every effort to keep the unity of the Spirit through the bond of peace. There is one body and one Spirit—just as you were called to one hope when you were called—one Lord, one faith, one baptism; one God and Father of all, who is over all and through all and in all" (Ephesians 4:1-6).

"Bear with each other and forgive whatever grievances you may have against one another. Forgive as the Lord forgave you. And over all these virtues put on love, which binds them all together in perfect unity. Let the peace of Christ rule in your hearts, since as members of one body you were called to peace. And be thankful" (Colossians 3:13-15).

It's impossible to read these passages—just a few among many throughout the Bible—and not be convinced that scriptural teaching focuses on unity among Christians. Unity is not incidental or secondary. Because it flows from our union with Christ, it goes down to the core of our identity as Christians. And because we are connected to Jesus, we are connected to each other. It is one of the great gifts Christians can experience in this life. It is the means by which we grow in our faith. It is a means for mission.

As Paul develops the metaphor of the "body of Christ," he makes it clear that Christians are all connected in powerful ways to Jesus Christ himself: therefore we are all connected to one another. To act as if we are not is deeply hurtful to the rest of the body; it is essentially self-mutilation of the body of Christ. These passages also reveal that the Scriptures are soberly aware of how difficult genuine unity is. They were written to churches (notably in Corinth) that were plagued by division and disunity. The Scriptures are never naive about unity. They look unflinchingly at the ugliness of disunity but never waver in calling people to the fullness, joy, and peace of being united in Christ.

Christianity—A Radically Unifying Faith

Many people are well-versed in the talking points of Christianity's intolerance and exclusivity—the Crusades, the Inquisition, bloodshed during the Reformation, Galileo's prison term, the Salem witch trials, colonial-era imperialism and missionary work, slavery as a biblically-sanctioned institution. Even the Holocaust sometimes gets laid at Christianity's feet. More recently, criticism has been aimed at Christianity's treatment of women and homosexuals. Some of these judgments are gross distortions of the truth and spectacularly unfair. While it's worth providing some helpful corrections and context for these assertions, it's perhaps even more valuable to demonstrate where Christianity has been an incredibly powerful force in advocating for human rights, healing deep divisions, and uniting previously warring factions.

Christian Unity Differs from Pop Culture Versions

Unity doesn't exist independently: it exists in, of, for, and around something else. While the culture makes unity an end, never really specifying *what exactly* we're supposed to be uniting around (because that might alienate some people), Christians make clear that the basis of our unity is the person and work of Jesus Christ. Paul says we are united in Christ (see Romans 6:5; Philippians 2:1). So Christian unity is in Christ, by Christ, and for Christ. He's clearly the cause, the reason, and the goal of our unity. To be a Christian is to live out our new identities as members of the body of Christ. So we are united *in* Christ and his gospel. Our unity is expressed in real community, and we are united around and for the mission.

Making our unity about Christ protects us from two common errors. The first error we sometimes make is embracing truth to the exclusion of unity. You know what this looks like—drawing a hard line at issues like eschatology, charismatic gifts, or Calvinist vs. Arminian. Sometimes it's an embrace of "our truth," as in our approach to Bible study, evangelism, or discipleship. This goes well beyond being passionate about a particular doctrine or distinctive to willfully breaking fellowship with other Bible-believing, Jesus-loving Christians because they view a certain issue differently. But if our unity is found in Christ, we ought to be humbled by the radical grace he extends to us in the gospel. We should be amazed that God would include us and be loathe to exclude anyone who loves the same savior we do.

The second error we tend to make is that of embracing unity to the exclusion of truth. This occurs when people make the mistake of believing that, because God's grace is accepting of all, anything goes. We need both grace and truth to have true unity. Jesus, in himself, personifies grace and truth, as the writer of Ephesians notes:

> Then we will no longer be infants, tossed back and forth by the waves, and blown here and there by every wind of teaching and by the cunning and craftiness of men in their deceitful scheming. Instead, speaking the truth in love, we will in all things grow up into him who is the Head, that is, Christ. From him the whole body, joined and held together by every supporting ligament, grows and builds itself up in love, as each part does its work. (Ephesians 4:14-16)

Why We Need Unity

We've already covered why unity is important from a biblical and cultural standpoint. We're well aware that Jesus prayed for it. You have probably talked and taught about it extensively in your ministry. But let's go further—into the missional reasons for unity. We need to be united in order to reach our campuses. Humble realism allows us to recognize that the mission is too big for any single group to reach the campus alone. But together, by the grace of God, we have a shot. Our unity must go beyond good feelings to embracing a shared mission. Lack of unity is directly linked to people missing out on saving faith. To overcome our lack of functional unity, we'll need to see that what (and who) we're losing is greater than what we gain by clinging to the status quo.

We need to be joined with the purpose of doing together what we could never do alone. We must go beyond the once-per-year event or campaign and work hard at united ministry during the other thirty or so weeks. Yes, the big events or service projects have their place, but partnership in the seemingly small stuff, like a weekly prayer meeting for a dozen or so leaders from different ministries, can go a long way.

Uniting in ministry doesn't mean collapsing into one big supergroup— far from it, in fact. Preserving our unique ministries, with their distinct personalities, emphases, strategies, and missional niches, is key to reaching the hundreds of people groups on our campuses. Quite often, unity efforts on campus exist to in some way turn all Christian groups into one big mouth. But the body of Christ is too diverse, too rich, and too beautiful for us to become reductionistic. We need to strive for unity on the other side of Christian diversity because there is tremendous value in having different groups that are able to reach different types of people but also work together.

Obstacles to Unity

Now that we have an idea what we're going for, let's talk about what gets in the way. With his usual bluntness, James diagnoses our problems:

> What causes fights and quarrels among you? Don't they come from your desires that battle within you? You want something but don't get it. You kill and covet, but you cannot have what you want. You quarrel and fight. You do not have, because you do not ask God. When you ask, you do not receive, because you ask with wrong motives, that you may spend what you get on your pleasures. (James 4:1-3)

It's easy to point fingers: "I'll tell you why ministries on our campus aren't united. Those guys!" It's not uncommon for ministers to keep a "book" on the practices and histories of certain groups to justify our aloofness toward them. But James says to start with ourselves and apply the gospel to these issues ("You want something but don't get it").

At the heart of disunity, we are fighting or "experiencing tension," as we like to diplomatically say. At the heart of disunity is our not getting something we want. What are we not getting? Here are a few common ones:

- Success—In terms of numbers or results, or however else we might define success, we fear the repercussions of "failure." So we say things like, "They say they have X number of students, but I heard it's not nearly that high."

- Feeling good about ourselves—We don't like the negative comparisons with others, and our pride would rather take others down a peg or two: "I'm not saying I'm the best teacher, but I'm not sure what people see in that leader. I went to a gathering once, and it seemed pretty fluffy/dry/milky/overly intellectual to me."

- Reputation—We let people into our successes, but not our failures or weaknesses. We carefully and craftily look for ways to embellish our stories and cause others to praise us. We crave the praise of people more than the blessing of God.

- Ambition—We feel that other people are standing in the way of our advancement and seek to work around or even against them, rather than with them. Instead of celebrating their victories, we begrudge them and enviously wish it were us instead.

If James is right, applying the gospel to our disunity will mean dealing with our heart motives. It will mean making sure that what we want, desire, and pray for really is aligned with God's kingdom purposes. It will mean cheering for others' success. It will mean finding our identity and self-worth not in our self-assessment, but in God's assessment of us. It will mean forsaking idols of reputation and not fearing what other people think of us. It will mean making sure our ambitions are primarily for God's kingdom, not our own.

How to Get There

Unity isn't cheap. The real thing can't be gained at a weekend ministry conference. It's a hard-fought struggle that is not achieved in a moment, but over years. True unity costs a lot, and the cost discourages many of us. It's hard to see immediate results, and the allocation of time and energy often seems incongruous to the results. It's true: in the short-term, unity is not "strategic." It may seem like you're giving time to meetings that don't lead to anything concrete, that you're giving more than you are receiving.

But this generosity sows the seeds that grow into things far exceeding what any of us can do alone.

Giving is a tangible check of our motives, of whether the gospel is at work. People who fight to get their own way, who are obsessed with their own reputation or ambitions, are not generous. So what are you giving away? Here are some worthwhile ways you can contribute to the kingdom-driven mission on your campus.

- Give something away! Offer your time, energy, and resources to others on campus with no expectation of return. Do an event without insisting your name get top billing or is even mentioned. Do it for Jesus. Be willing to let your individual or organizational kingdom shrink so God's kingdom can expand.
- Pray for it! Don't simply pray for one another, but pray for your unity. Open up your group's prayer times to people from other groups while also prioritizing united prayer efforts that aren't "owned" by any particular group.
- Tithe your time. Build into your weekly schedule efforts toward unity. Time together builds up trust. Conversation and prayer lead to opportunities. Regular communication allows everyone to minister more effectively (a case in point being communication about students who float between several ministries).
- If you're on a big campus with many ministries or if you're on a campus with a history of some bad blood, rivalry, or strained relationships, meaningful unity may not be immediately possible. Work more intentionally with a handful to model to the rest of the body what it could be. Keep at the forefront the goal of including more people as you seek out providential partnerships, often across traditional boundary lines.
- Assess your ministry model. Could you find a niche for yourself that reaches a different group of students, that doesn't dilute the pool of Christian students? Could you change how you do things in order to not dilute or reinvent what someone else is already doing, but reach more students?

- Map the campus. Talking and planning could allow you to see where resources are focused and where they aren't. Map the campus for Bible studies/small groups, large group meetings, and where certain people groups tend to gather. You may find that one dorm features Bible studies from six different groups, while the dorm next door has only one. Mapping will allow everyone to work smarter and more effectively.
- Read through the "Chicago Agreement," a document signed by a number of campus ministry organizations. It is included below, as a starting point. Consider sharing it with other group leaders as you begin or continue to move toward unity for one common goal.

Chicago Agreement: Unity in Mission

As ministries committed to the Gospel of Jesus Christ and united in his mission on college campuses, the following groups listed below met on October 25, 2010 and agreed to teach the staff, volunteers, faculty and student leadership of our organizations the following principles about relationships with other Christian groups. (John 13: 34 & 35)

1. We are all part of Christ's body.
2. We do not regard any campus as our exclusive field. We recognize that many students and faculty may be helped through the various appeals and styles of the different organizations.
3. We will seek to establish relationships and build bridges with our counterparts in other Christian groups on campus. When establishing ministries on new campuses, we will take the initiative to communicate with the leadership of existing groups.
4. We will speak well of and refrain from criticism of each others' ministries and members.
5. We commit to addressing problems on a local, regional or national level by humbly communicating with our counterparts, seeking the Lord together to resolve the issues.
6. We affirm the leadership commitments students and faculty have made to each others' ministries and will not actively recruit them away from those groups. When starting a new campus work, each organization will endeavor to select new leaders, not leaders from other ministries.
7. We recognize students and faculty have the freedom to choose their involvement with any campus ministry. In general, we will encourage them to select and be involved with one primary organization.
8. We will encourage collaborative efforts on a voluntary basis between our organizations. We are open to share experiences and resources to assist each other with the unique challenges of campus ministry.

Chapter 12

CHURCH, PARACHURCH, AND THE THIRD WAY OF MISSIONAL CAMPUS MINISTRY

To love Jesus is to love his Church—

all *of it.*

Have you ever had conversations with students like this? "I like (unnamed ministry's) weekly meeting. I like the sermons. I like the worship time. It's my church." Of course, it's *not* a local church; it's a weekly campus fellowship group meeting. And I know that if the leaders of that ministry were there, they would emphatically deny that their weekly meeting is a church! They would affirm their commitment to being a part of a local church. Still, conversations like this one are repeated on my campus, and probably yours, hundreds of times each semester.

When it comes to campus ministry, questions of who should be leading the charge inevitably arise: The local church? Parachurch? Should they work together? *Can* they work together? Do these distinctions even matter? My answer to all these questions is *yes*. In this chapter I will discuss the dominant paradigms in campus ministry and the need for a third way.

Defining Parachurch and Church

For any of you who are unclear about what these terms mean, it might be helpful to define them. Parachurch ministries are those that operate outside of the oversight of local churches or denominations. The college ministry world is home to some of the best-known parachurch ministries around, such as Campus Crusade for Christ, InterVarsity, and Navigators. They are part of the church universal. The prefix *para* means "to come alongside," so theoretically these ministries come alongside the local church for a particular purpose.

When we say "local church," we mean a particular congregation of Christians, gathered for worship, community, and mission. This doesn't *have* to mean a church building with a steeple, pastor, choir or contemporary worship rock band, though both churched and unchurched people often have very "churchy" assumptions about what church should be. During the Reformation, when the Protestants were getting kicked out of the Roman Catholic Church right and left, the question of what defines a church was a pressing one. They arrived at a simple definition, identifying three "marks:" the preaching of the gospel, the proper administration of the sacraments, and the right exercise of church discipline.[1]

While this definition is helpful (and I believe true), it also creates a host of questions, such as Who gets to preach? (and what qualifies as preaching?), What are the sacraments, and who gets to administer them?, What is church discipline, and who exercises that? The history of Protestantism is about churches (and other ministries) answering these questions and others in different—and diverging—ways. For example, in which category would you place denominationally affiliated college ministries such as Baptist Collegiate Ministries (Southern Baptist Convention), Chi Alpha (Assembly of God), Reformed University Fellowship (Presbyterian Church in America), Association of Collegiate Ministries (Christian Churches), or Wesley Foundation (United Methodist)? Are these ministries of the local church? Are they extensions of a local church or a denomination? Are they parachurch ministries, operating within the sphere of a particular denomination? Are they simply the church but with a different location and look? Even these ministries—which operate in similar ways once on campus—answer these questions differently. This brings us immediately into the area of ecclesiology.

Ecclesiology

Ecclesiology is the theology and study of the Church. It comes from the New Testament Greek word for church, *ekklesia*, or "assembly." As we know, the church is not a place, but a people. Why bring this up regarding college ministry? Because much of college ministry happens at the intersection of campus, church, and parachurch, and our field has provided some of the more vexing issues in ecclesiology for a couple generations.

What's the ideal relationship between campus, church, and parachurch, and what's our theology regarding each entity? These questions are important because our functional theology leads to our practice. Our ecclesiology—whether it's worked out or not, whether we are conscious of it or not—will have a direct impact on what we do. We must address real questions, such as:

- Are church and parachurch partners, or should they have "sphere sovereignty?"

- Regarding parachurch, is there something inherently illegitimate about its existence (as some charge)?
- Regarding church, should it defer to the parachurch's unique calling and equipping for on-campus ministry?
- How can the local church most effectively serve and reach out to students? Is that its job?
- How actively should parachurch ministries be making local church involvement a priority?
- Is my Bible study or fellowship group a church? Why/why not?

These are just a few of the questions that come up. We can't answer all of them now, but we can agree that they are important and often divisive in our efforts to reach out to campuses. And we can begin to address them by working toward a better relationship between church and parachurch in our mission to the campus.

Dominant Paradigms

Two paradigms have dominated—and even competed in—campus ministry: the first is the "let the (local) church do it" approach (often a large, resourced church). The second is the "let the parachurch do it" approach (often large, nationally and internationally known, with an array of staff and pre-packaged resources and events). Unfortunately, as someone who has served as both a pastor in a church and as a campus minister with a parachurch organization, I've seen many cases in which the dominant paradigms don't work that well, but where a third way approach is bearing tremendous fruit.

The Local Church

Local churches often view campus ministry as something that happens within their four walls. If the church has a good reputation and resources, it can attract students and may be able to gather a decent crowd. In the best scenario, students are regularly reminded that the body of Christ is more diverse than eighteen- to twenty-two-year-old college students. In age-diverse churches, students are recipients of teaching, counsel, and hospitality from older members of the church. They also have the opportunity to jump in and serve the church in its various ministries and mission.

But in far too many churches, this isn't the case. Instead, students show up for services and are funneled to age-segmented gatherings where the only people they connect with are other college students. They find it difficult to get involved because few churches are geared to involve in meaningful ways the constantly shifting mass of students. In this scenario, how missional is the church? While it is essential for Christian students to have a spiritual home during their college years, we must ask whether the church is doing enough to reach the campus.

Simply being "student friendly" is not an effective strategy for reaching non-Christian students. As we move further into a post-Christian society, it becomes far less likely that an unchurched non-Christian will enter a local church in search of God. Local churches may have great intentions but often lack resourcing, know-how, staffing, and national networking. When this is the case, they undermine Christian students' mission to their campus by removing them from it.

Parachurch Ministries

The second paradigm is that of the parachurch campus ministry, which views college ministry as their specialty. Parachurch campus ministry arose because of the void created by churches' collective inability, unwillingness, or ambivalence to reach out to students. In the best scenario, a parachurch ministry is able to reach students with the gospel and connect them to a body of Christian students. They receive regular, relevant teaching uniquely suited to their context and lifestage. They worship and serve with other Christians and incarnate Christ in all the corners of the campus. Buoyed by this experience during their college years, they make their way to meaningful involvement in a church beyond graduation.

But a parachurch ministry can just as easily fall short of the ideal. For decades, observers have noted the ease with which parachurch fellowship groups create Christian ghettos, where instead of being a community of missionaries to their campus, they act as hermetically sealed bubbles of

Christian culture. The fellowship group becomes little more than a haven for people who "think like me, speak like me, dress like me." Too many ministries even state that their purpose is to be little more than a "safe place," a place to babysit churched kids and "protect" them from the world.

Adding to these problems is the phenomenon of parachurch-without-local-church. Parachurch ministries may encourage their students to be involved in a local church but leave no room for actual church involvement in their philosophy of ministry or weekly planning. Consequently, students are discipled in a lifestyle of churchless Christianity. Upon graduation, they look for a setting just like their fellowship group; when they find none, they "graduate" from meaningful involvement in the body of Christ.

We can all rehearse the failings of the other side: "We would like to connect our students to churches, but churches just don't get campus ministry. They don't understand college students like we do. Students get lost in the shuffle there." Or, "Campus ministries aren't equipped and networked like we are. They work in isolation and drain needed resource from the local church. They don't adequately train their staff or prepare students for a lifetime of following Christ."

There's enough truth to these claims that we can't simply dismiss them. We also can't be hardened by them because we need each other, but our need for each other doesn't address *how* we work together. For example, traditional churches have long been uncomfortable about the roles parachurch have assumed while the parachurch has responded with "at least we're doing something. At least we're on mission." But new critiques of parachurch are emerging.

Parasitic Parachurch?

In his book *Organic Leadership*, Neil Cole lays a heavy charge at the feet of the parachurch, calling for an end to their "parasitical" practices. While Cole does not condemn all parachurch organizations or practices, he is concerned with how the parachurch has largely taken over tasks that also belong to the Church to the point of making her (the Church) weak and unhealthy. Consider the following from Cole:

- Her leadership development has been assumed by colleges, seminaries, and Bible institutes.
- Her compassion and social justice have been given over to non-profit charitable organizations.
- Her global mission has been relinquished to mission agencies.
- Church government and decision making have often been forfeited to denominational offices.
- Her prophetic voice has been replaced by publishing houses, self-help gurus, and futurist authors.
- Her emotional and spiritual health has been taken over by psychologists, psychiatrists, and family counseling services.

The world today looks at the church wondering what relevance she has. The only use they see for the church is performing the sacerdotal duties of preaching, marrying, burying, baptizing, and passing around wafers and grape juice. The church was once a catalyst for artistic expression, social change, and the founding of hospitals, schools, and missionary enterprise, but today she has settled for providing a one-hour-a-week worship concert, an offering place, and a sermon.[2]

To Cole's list above, I would add that "her local mission to college campuses has been outsourced to college ministries." Is this outsourcing biblical, and missional? And what are we to make of a parachurch ministry that takes the resources of a local church to do the job the local church could be doing, all while not feeding and strengthening the local church? Cole's critique has merit. For those of us who operate as part of the universal church, we should be making it clear to those we serve and especially empower that we are just that—a *part* of the body. If we invite students to be a part of what we're doing, it is key that we communicate the provisional and particular nature of our purpose.

The Third Way: A Complementarian Approach

Because of the shortcomings of our current approaches to campus ministry, we need a "third way" of campus-church connection. Instead of thinking that college ministry consists of getting students to merely attend a church, instead of outsourcing college ministry to parachurch ministries, *a missional campus ministry approach utilizes the strengths of parachurch ministries to empower the local church to take its place on the missional edge.* I call this approach *complementarian.*

I'm borrowing this term from the ongoing conversation in the evangelical world over gender roles in the home and church. Egalitarians believe that because men and women are of equal worth as people created in the image of God (a point with which no Bible-believing Christian disagrees), that therefore women should be able to *do* everything a man does. Complementarians believe that men and women are equal but have different God-ordained functions in the home and church: because their differences are real, and they are designed for each other, they *complement* each other. To regard them as the same would be to rob each of their distinctives. In the same way, I believe local church and parachurch need to recognize and celebrate their differences as they work together.

Of crucial importance to conversations on both gender and ecclesiology is the question of who has authority, who takes the lead. In terms of our ecclesiology conversation, many parachurch ministries are functionally egalitarians, even as they espouse complementarian values. They may be doing an incredible job on campus but robbing the local church of its ability and opportunity to embrace its sent-ness. A missional church is a sent church. For churches with campuses nearby, those students are their neighbors, and there should be a sense in which loving them will send them *to* the campus. This means that they must be present on campus, physically and frequently, that they must seek to contextualize the gospel to the people group of college students. A missional church strives to speak the language as they disciple the students to be missionaries on and to their campus.

The local church does not stop with a successful ministry on campus but instead builds a bridge between church and campus, making room for students to participate fully in the life of their church so students are both served and serving in meaningful ways. In a post-Christian world, this is a crucial way for the church to enter into and engage culture as at the same time they make disciples for a lifetime.

What of parachurch ministries, then? Emphasizing the church's place on the missional edge does not diminish or dismiss the important roles of parachurch ministries. Rather, it allows them to recover their true calling to "come alongside" the Church, to facilitate, resource, and equip the Church for *its* mission. Parachurch college ministries have decades of experience in reaching students. They have national networks for gathering them and resourcing ministry to them. As a result, they can act as translators and campus-missionary trainers. And while they can certainly take the lead, if there's ever a question of authority, they should willingly defer to the local church.

Parachurch ministries ought to adopt a John the Baptist role: prepare the way, and then be willing to get out of the way. Be willing to step back and to decrease in reputation. If a local church is taking its place on the missional edge, be willing to help facilitate, even if another person or group is receiving the credit. When parachurch organizations operate this way, we're no longer unhealthy parasites: we become part of symbiotic, healthy, life-giving, complementary relationships. Building vibrant ministry on campus while creating meaningful connection to a local church is the most fruitful way we can see college students become Christ-centered laborers and followers for life. A missional campus ministry will not see students graduate from the body of Christ because they will already be meaningfully connected to the body in all her messy glory.

As we move rapidly into a post-Christian era, we must work to repair the burned bridges and cold distances between church and parachurch organizations on our campuses—and soon. I believe the North American Church in all its forms will be shaken and refined. Many will fall by the wayside or linger on only as shells of their former selves; but what remains will be stronger and will have a clearer sense of mission. No longer content to simply outsource campus ministry to the parachurch, I believe missional churches will be (and already are) more proactive in taking their place on the front lines of campus ministry. We are already seeing this with many of the most innovative and fruitful churches in North America today.

Loving the Church in *All* Her Forms

Why is it so difficult for church and parachurch organizations to work well together? Pride is the chief sin, the foundational sin, the sin that lies underneath all others. Pick up the rocks of suspicion, disdain, lack of trust, or selfish independence, and we will find pride wriggling underneath. It is pride that destroys otherwise fruitful partnerships between church and parachurch. It is pride that causes turf issues, that makes us see the other with disdain, that results in disunity and unfruitfulness, and that deeply grieves Jesus.

We must continue going back to the gospel. Our righteousness and identity are not found in what we *do* in ministry but in what Jesus has accomplished for us. Laying our ministries at the cross, as acts of worship, should melt our pride, humble us, and make us thankful that Jesus calls us to partner with him in his work. Jesus not only reconciles us to God, but to one another, for the sake of his mission.

If you love Jesus, you should love his bride—the Church. Jesus died for the Church, and it's for the Church that Jesus is coming back. To love Jesus is to love his Church—*all* of it. So how can we express the appropriate love for and to the Church? We can love each other, and we can work together in the mission we've been given. So let's get to work. Let's repent of our sinful attitudes and actions, and look for meaningful ways to partner together in order to see the kingdom come in power on our campuses.

What Does Loving the Church Look Like?

I can't lay out four easy steps to forming partnerships because our churches and ministries vary so much. A missional mindset always takes into account the need to work out the particulars of our ministries onsite. However, we can talk about the *values* that shape the partnership of local church and parachurch.

I. View both local church and parachurch as part of God's redemptive plan.

Recognize and appreciate your need for the other. As parts of the body of Christ, we suffer when every part isn't doing its divinely ordained work—so embrace our symbiotic (not parasitic) relationship. Jesus said, "'It is more blessed to give than to receive'" (Acts 20:35). This idea should guide our interactions with each other. Our ministries ought to exist in a constant feedback loop. People need fellowship and a safe place to grow, but these are not ends in themselves. The local church, or campus ministry, has much bigger goals than its own self-preservation: we are to be ministries on a mission. But neither is church or our fellowship *merely* a means to mission. Rather, they feed into and support each other.

2. Recognize that students need the local church.

Because college ministry is not just about the here and now but about preparation for life, it is preferable that students connect to the body in all its diversity—young and old, married and single, educated and non-educated—as opposed to only connecting with other eighteen- to twenty-two-year-olds who are just like them. If students don't see now that their mission as Christians will always involve the Church, they won't be missional for life. A good church will model to the students what it means to be missional.

It's imperative that this value touches down in the day-to-day reality of college ministry life. It must be modeled by the staff and in key decision-making. That we value the local church should show up on the calendar, in the budget, and in staffing decisions. It's one thing to say, "Yes, get involved in a local church." It's another to model our ministry in such a way as to do everything we can to ensure it actually happens. Here are four qualities I look for in a church before I recommend it to students:

1. It clearly preaches the gospel.
2. It's local. We want students to be missional where they are, not commuting home every weekend. The closer to campus, and the easier for them to get there, the better.

3. It seeks to be missional in its context and to meaningfully involve students in its mission.

4. Other students are meaningfully involved in it.

3. Recognize that the local church needs students—and their college ministers.

Connecting students to the local church is imperative for the survival, health, and growth of the church. College-age students and twentysomethings in general are an often neglected, unreached, and under-utilized part of the body of Christ, but their unique combination of faith, maturity, flexibility, and relative freedom makes them an incredibly potent kingdom force. When they are challenged rather than babied, when they have an empowering and compelling call, they often surprise their elders in how they step up.

They can be a great blessing and source of life and energy to a local church. But in order to bless and energize a church, the church body must be willing and humble enough to meaningfully include students in the life of the church. Humility is required in order to acknowledge that the church not only welcomes students but can *learn* from them. When a church reaches this conclusion, space is made for students to serve on its ministry teams, and mere attendance is discouraged (of course, this requires a church that is already missional in orientation, with a pre-existing culture of "sentness").

The local church also needs its campus ministry staff. It's not uncommon to hear excuses like, "I don't serve here—this is where I get fed." But that's an unbiblical, unmissional view of the local church. The local church should be where we are fed and where we feed others. Ministering on campus does not make us exempt from jumping in along with everyone else with whom we are on mission.

Chapter 13
MINISTRY AT THE GLOBAL UNIVERSITY

Change the university and you change the world.[1]

—Charles Habib Malik

D. L. Moody, a nineteenth-century American evangelist, publisher, and the founder of Moody Bible Institute, once said, "Water runs downhill and the highest hills are the great cities. If we can stir them we shall stir the whole country."[2] I believe the same can be said of college campuses around the world. Many of them are global cities in microcosm, and through them we can reach many nations of the world at once. We stir the world by stirring the campuses, and we do this by starting missional ministries and churches that reach college campuses.

The Global City

In recent years, students of business, culture, and politics have observed that the world is "flattening," creating a truly international community and making national borders less important. One of the results of this phenomenon is the emergence of the "global city" or "world city." The global city is defined as a city or metropolitan area that acts as a major node in international commercial, social, and technological networks. What happens in and through a global city has a direct and tangible effect on the rest of the world in a variety of spheres. In addition, global cities often have more in common with each other than with those in their own country.

In 1999, GaWC (the Globalization and World City Research Network, based at Loughborough University) awarded their highest global city rating to New York, London, Paris, and Tokyo. A second tier included Chicago, Frankfurt, Hong Kong, Los Angeles, Milan, and Singapore. Many other cities are recognized as being global in some respect, which means they meet these agreed-upon characteristics of a global city:

- Name recognition—stating what country or state the city is in is unnecessary
- Large population—center of at least one million but typically several million
- Diverse—along racial, ethnic, socioeconomic, and cultural lines
- Commerce and finance—flow of major capital and employment through multi-national corporations and financial institutions
- Culture shaping—renowned art, film, music, theater scenes

- Political influence—what happens there matters elsewhere
- Major academic center—universities and colleges, some of which are also global
- Advanced infrastructure—mass transit, airports, telecommunications
- Major sporting center—multiple teams, arenas and stadiums, ability to host international sporting events

The culture-shaping influence of global cities has accelerated with the effects of globalization and technology. Those at the highest levels of commerce, culture, and politics have long recognized that there is no more strategic place than the global city, and this is also true in ministry. Churches are important everywhere, but the most strategic places to plant churches are in the cities, and the most strategic cities are those with global influence. To reach the rest of the world, we must start by reaching global cities. Some of the most missionally-minded leaders in the church today are structuring their ministries to do just this. It's my belief that successful missional ministry efforts will in turn first focus their attention on global universities.

The Global University

The global university (also an entity recognized by those studying global cities) may be thought of as a global city in microcosm in terms of its makeup, its culture, and its influence. Global university characteristics mirror those of the global city:

- Name recognition—one- or two-word names that need no explanation, such as Harvard, Yale, Princeton
- Size—large (often more than 20,000 students), or residing in or near a large metropolitan area
- Academic excellence—not restricted to Ivy League, this includes the number of published articles by faculty, Rhodes scholars, and other similar criteria
- Diverse population—including international students (more on this below)
- Influential—culturally, politically, and intellectually

- Destination for multi-national companies—flow of capital for research and employment
- Major sporting centers—in the U.S., the NCAA is a billion dollar industry

Using this criteria, a number of surveys have attempted to rank global universities. Their lists include not only the most obvious schools (Harvard, Cambridge, Yale, Oxford, Stanford, Princeton), but also some less expected ones, such as the University of Illinois, the University of Wisconsin, the University of Texas—Austin, the University of Pittsburgh, Purdue University, and Penn State University, among others.[3] While there is certainly some variation from list to list, the importance in reaching students on these campuses and those like them across the country—and the world—remains.

The diversity of the students we'll find on these campuses provides undeniable evidence that by reaching college students we'll reach the rest of the world. The world is coming to study in the U.S. in record numbers. Over the past three decades, the number of foreign students (those whose citizenship is in another country) in higher education has grown more than fourfold: from 600,000 worldwide in 1975 to 2.7 million in 2004.[4] The U.S. hosts the largest percentage of these foreign students of any nation, at 22 percent, or 594,000, which means that international students make up approximately 3.5 percent of the total higher education population.[5] This number may initially seem relatively insignificant, but keep in mind two factors: many of these students are graduate—not undergraduate—students, where they make up an even higher percentage of those seeking advanced degrees. Also, many of them are the elite of their respective countries, to which they will return in significant positions of leadership and influence.

Ministry to the Global Universities

Given their unique influence, global universities are perhaps the most strategic mission field in the world. Although all campus ministry is certainly important, ministries that prioritize staffing, funding, and resourcing to these universities will most likely be more fruitful in evangelizing to the rest of the world than universities that have less influence. Effective campus ministry can serve as a predictor for what will be successful in the cities: what has been fruitful at global universities will likely be fruitful in the global cities and should be observed by those engaged in ministry there. In the same way, campus ministers working at global universities can model their efforts after those that have been successful in reaching global cities.

The following elements are necessary for effectively ministering to the global universities but are also true for those who are ministering on smaller campuses in North America:

1. Amid secular unbelief, faithfully proclaim and incarnate the orthodox gospel

The gospel is as offensive as it has ever been to unbelievers, tempting students, and even ministries, to soften the blunt edges, blur distinctions, and otherwise take the bargain offered by relativism: "You leave us alone, and we'll leave you alone." In our current context, Christians must engage non-Christians and their questions in a humble, respectful, informed manner. These opportunities exist in thousands of informal conversations every day, as well as in more official forums, including class and special events.

Most Western, college-going non-Christians consider themselves to be "beyond" organized religion, while also believing they have examined Christianity and found it wanting. In this environment, it's crucial that we clearly and repeatedly engage them with the gospel until it's clear to non-Christians that Christianity isn't at all what they thought it was.

2. Amid the transience and hyper-mobility of "emerging adulthood," challenge students to stay after graduation and renew their campus and city

Students often treat their campuses as rest stops on the highway to the rest of their lives. It is essential to emphasize that life does not begin later but *now*. When students are given a Jeremiah 29 vision for campus and community renewal, we find they are uniquely equipped, before and after graduation, to reach their global campus and/or city with the gospel.

To overcome the tendency to move on, it is essential that college students form a strong connection to their local church, going beyond simply attending services to being meaningfully involved. Church leadership must be open to students' involvement, casting a vision for their role in seeing the church advance and the kingdom come. Campus ministry staff should actively seek to bring students into their local church and continue shepherding those students as they become involved in the church. It is my hope that working with and among college students will begin to be seen as a viable and strategic church planting strategy and one that will bear considerable fruit in renewing entire cities.

3. Amid diversity and pluralism, contextualize ministry to many different types of people and worldviews

A survey of campus ministry resources reveals the assumption that college students all basically believe the same thing. But students are not monolithic. It would be nice if this were true, and perhaps it was at one time. But now this assumption is reductionistic and simply untrue. On a typical campus, we are likely to find several different worldview people groups: traditional and conservative people (often from the Bible Belt areas); modern-thinking people (disproportionately found in the sciences); postmodern-thinking people (still predominant in the arts and humanities); and a fourth group, what we could call post-postmodern, for lack of a better term.

Recognizing that postmodernity is bankrupt, in part because of its inability to call anything evil, those in academia and pop culture have been pointing to something new—what has also been called hyper-modernity, pseudo-modernity, trans-modernity, and "The New Sincerity." It is unclear if this will cohere into anything or how exactly it will change our thinking, but it *is* clear that orienting ministry to only one worldview will not reach the diverse people groups on the typical global university campus.

4. Amid the pressures of the larger culture and the errors of subculture on the one hand and cultural assimilation on the other, create a countercultural community

We've already discussed college ministries' tendencies to serve as little more than bunkers for Christian students to hide from campus culture. In doing so, they mirror the posture of many churches in North America. Some others, in the search for relevance, are not much different from campus culture. Both have lost the uniquely Christian character of dynamic, outward-facing engagement without conformity.

Forming a countercultural community is essential in order to disciple believers and witness to non-Christians. It is in the context of this community that the gospel is worked into every area of life. This means radically departing from cultural approaches to sex, money, power, school, work, and entertainment. Christians recognize all of these as gifts but in the freedom of the gospel, seek to neither abuse nor idolize them as culture does.

This countercultural community moves beyond fellowship and accountability to partnership in engaging and renewing the campus culture at large. The posture of this community is to respectfully and humbly engage the larger culture to bless, renew, and redeem it. Renewing the campus requires unity and kingdom-centered prayer among Christians. Ministries must move beyond the rivalry of competing for students' attention. They must also move beyond busyness, in which they are so absorbed in their own ministry that they have no time for communication with their co-laborers.

Instead of mirroring the hyper-individualistic autonomy, fragmentation, and alienation of the culture at large, Christian ministries seek active partnership, mutuality, and communication. Jesus said that the church in complete unity would demonstrate his identity and mission to the world. In a world that hungers for unity because we see so little, churches and ministries that refuse to partner with one another willingly prop up one of the greatest objections to the gospel.

5. Amid the compartmentalization of faith to one, private area of life, integrate faith into all of life

Unfortunately, much of campus ministry focuses only on the inner, "spiritual" life and does not take seriously the need to shepherd students through the faith and intellect crises that are common in the college years. In the absence of counsel and discipleship, students often create a false dichotomy between faith and intellect. This is a disservice to them and a defeater of Christian belief to non-Christians.

This counterculture equips students to think, speak, and live as Christians in all areas of life, addressing the use and abuse of authority, sexuality and relationships, and especially work and the intellect. To effectively engage our audience, our missional approaches to campus ministry must be unashamedly, rigorously intellectual.

6. Amid great suffering and injustice in the world and the hunger for reconciliation, be actively engaged in ministries of mercy and justice

This generation of students is globally aware and engaged: they are a generation of activists. When we work for mercy and justice alongside non-Christians, we become co-advocates with them in combating poverty, human trafficking, climate change, and so on. However, we must remember that our motive in working for justice should differ from the motives of secular (or spiritual) non-Christians. As Christians, we are joining with God in his mission to renew and restore the world, to put things right. Despite their noble motives to alleviate suffering, non-Christians have no such hope to glorify God. Instead, they are often motivated by underlying spiritual and philosophical belief systems that have set themselves up in opposition to the gospel.

In this context, we must be mindful that we do not substitute the social gospel for the gospel. The gospel is certainly a holistic gospel, and Jesus' proclamation of the arrival of the kingdom included the alleviation of suffering. But the kingdom that alleviates suffering arrived through the word and deed of Jesus Christ. The gospel of Jesus Christ as Savior and Lord must be proclaimed. To do any less than this is not faithful to the gospel. If our efforts for mercy and justice are not authentic, proceeding from hearts that genuinely desire Christ's reign and rule to come, we will be dismissed as hypocrites.

Conclusion

Former President of the United Nations General Assembly (and Christian) Charles Habib Malik was a Lebanese philosopher, theologian, and diplomat. In his famous address "A Christian Critique of the University," Harvard-educated Malik spoke prophetically about the importance of reaching the University:

> The University is a clear-cut fulcrum with which to move the world. The problem here is for the church to realize that no greater service can it render both itself and the cause of the gospel, with which it is entrusted, than to try to recapture the universities for Christ on whom they were all originally founded. One of the best ways of treating the macrocosm is through the handle of the universities in which millions of youths destined to positions of leadership spend, in rigorous training, between four and ten years of the most formative period of their life. More potently than by any other means, change the university and you change the world.[6]

In the era of the global city and the global university, this message is truer than ever.

Chapter 14
OPEN TO THE FUTURE

Any customer can have a car painted any colour
that he wants so long as it is black.[1]

—Henry Ford's remark about the Model T

Henry Ford changed the world with the Model T automobile. His innovations in engineering, development, and distribution revolutionized the world and the way we live in it. He was a legend in his own time, but he became so obsessed with his invention that it nearly ruined his company. Ford was fiercely tenacious about clinging to his ideas. On one occasion, while Ford was on vacation, his engineers completely updated the Model T into a low-slung, shiny red model. When he returned, they proudly showed it to him. One observer recalled,

> He had his hands in his pockets, and he walked around the car three or four times, looking at it very closely . . . Finally, he got to the left-hand side of the car that was facing me, and he takes his hands out, gets hold of the door, and bang! He ripped the door right off! How the man done it, I don't know![2]

Without saying a word, Ford ripped the car apart, piece by piece, until he destroyed it—*with his bare hands*. The message was clear: there would be no innovation. They would *always* do things the boss's way.

At certain crucial moments in Church history, ministry for and by college students has led the Church in prayerfully re-envisioning ministry for the world. It's my conviction that campus ministry must again become an incubator for reaching our post-Christian world. It ought to serve as a laboratory for ministry, experimenting in how to reach an ever-shifting culture with the eternal gospel. Campus ministry is uniquely positioned to shape the future because we work with those who *are* the future.

In this moment, the world is rapidly changing all around us. Today, we take for granted technologies we didn't dream of only a few years ago. Beliefs and morality that were frowned upon in the not-so-distant past are accepted. The only constant is change, and campus ministry should be keeping pace. We work with the generation that is living the future right now. We dare not become stale, predictable, or cliché.

It's easy to become like Henry Ford in campus ministry. Though we start off full of fire and willing to take risks, eventually we arrive upon a formula that works, and we stick with it. Before we know it, we're blindly ripping apart the changes we need to be making so we can thrive in the future. We don't know for sure what the future will hold (though I've taken some stabs at predicting what it could look like later in this chapter), but we *do* know we need to be open to the future. Openness is a missional imperative simply because people and culture are always changing.

By being open to the future, we can avoid puttering around in our Model Ts while the rest of the world speeds past us. As campus ministers, it's imperative that we stay in the loop. Theologian Karl Barth famously stated that it was wise to begin the day with the Bible in one hand and a newspaper in the other.[3] Now, many of us integrate all our Scriptural and news resources into our laptop or smartphone: how ever we learn, it's imperative for campus ministers to work at being active learners every day. In doing so, we develop personally, professionally, and missionally.

We work with students and institutions that highly value knowledge. A fully incarnational and faithful ministry should be constantly building a knowledge base. When we're consistently reading, associating, and connecting the dots, we build our credibility with those we are serving. Being active learners opens doors to new opportunities. It helps us learn and listen. It helps us remember what our students are (supposed to be) doing much of the time they're not meeting with us. It helps us feel that we too are part of this learning community called a university.

With limitless information literally at our fingertips, the potential for information overload is real—which is why we should do our learning, thinking, and innovating in community. If we are open to new ideas, as well as open with our ideas, we will all be better off for it. If we want to be effective college ministers, we will give our colleagues and students permission to try new things—and permission to fail. We will be transparent and waste less time in meetings not relevant to us, instead getting more involved in areas in which we're skilled and about which we're passionate.

One mark of being open to the future is that we embrace the speed of change. Instead of trying to build a static program or institution, we build a fluid, dynamic movement. Students change, schools change, cultures change—so should we. While we shouldn't fear the future, it is wise to have an understanding of how our world is changing and to be prepared for what we may be dealing with in a few years.

Disruptions That Could Shake Up College Ministry

In the early 2000s, the United States Postal Service was stable. They delivered millions of pieces of mail, and that number stayed relatively unchanged from year to year. Meanwhile, revenue was increasing. But starting in 2006, the USPS experienced a major reduction in the level of volume—down 17 percent since 2006. Now, the service is struggling to adapt to the new landscape.

What happened? The USPS was surprised by a disruption event. They saw stable volume and increasing revenue but missed the fact that competitors were gaining on them and larger forces were aligned against them. As package delivery systems and standards have changed and the number of letters being sent has decreased dramatically in a digital age, the USPS is struggling to hold on.

It is my conviction that the field of college ministry could be headed for its own disruption event in the next five to ten years. We can rarely predict the future, let alone control it. But we can prepare for it. Rather than simply reacting, we can take a proactive posture toward coming changes. As people who work with younger generations, we straddle the present and the future. We should be the early adopters and the best adapters to coming changes. Why? Because one person's disruption event is another person's golden opportunity.

While I certainly can't predict the exact changes that will reshape the Church and college ministry, here are five that I believe have seismic potential. Each of them would mean a serious challenge to the status quo of college ministry:

1. The Higher Ed bubble will burst.

The rapid growth of Higher Ed was built on the largest cohort of college students ever, plus years of low-interest rate student loans. But that was before the Great Recession. With tuition costs at an all-time high, and loan obligations stretching out longer and longer, people are increasingly wondering if college is worth it. Institutions themselves are over-extended and making cuts. The system as we know it may not be sustainable for much longer.

The promise of college for everyone is increasingly out of reach. We may be looking at a massive constriction—fewer students, perhaps even fewer institutions. What if we have significantly fewer students coming to school because of economic considerations? What if the students who are no longer coming are the relatively poor, disenfranchised ones? In this scenario, it's easy to imagine Higher Ed returning to its elitist roots. If this happens, it will have huge implications on the "who" and "how" of ministry. We'll have to adapt to working with two diverging swaths of the population—those who are privileged and still able to access college and those who are struggling to get by while in school. Both groups present challenges to our extracurricular model.

2. Technology (and other cultural forces) will distance, disperse, and depersonalize connection to students.

One of my extended family members is a University of Central Florida student, but he doesn't frequent campus all that often: in fact, during one recent semester he took all five of his classes online. Students like him are becoming more and more common. The rise of online learning is a profitable boon for Higher Ed, but it's not an unmixed blessing. The lower cost and easy accessibility of online higher education make gaining a college degree easier for older students with families or those who can't afford living and learning on campus. But among many things, online students miss out on gathering as a group in a classroom, learning not only from their professors but from their peers.

Online learning hasn't been around long enough to really research its implications on society, but just for a moment imagine that thousands of students *aren't* descending on a nearby campus every August. What if thousands of freshmen *aren't* trying to navigate that campus? Or more pointedly, what if they are enrolled but are spread all over the world, taking classes on their laptop from their bedroom? What if the university no longer provided our ministries with the "service" of gathering and centralizing the student body? How would we connect with them? How would we serve them? How would we minister to them and equip them for ministry?

This is yet another notable strike against attractional ministry. Attractional ministry can work if there are large masses of students to attract. As it is, the number of churched kids is already shrinking. If traditional student feeder systems recede to only a trickle, many current ministry models may not be sustainable. These changes will also push our field even further in creative development of missional, outward-facing, externally-focused campus ministry. If the students don't come to us, we'll have to go to them. We'll have to look harder to find them. And we'll likely have to adopt new measurements for success, as our ministries will have many more meetings with smaller groups of students—ministries that may be just as decentralized and fragmented as the student bodies they serve.

We'll have to transition from an emphasis on gathering to an emphasis on granular ministry, from macro to micro, from getting a thousand students to our location to equipping students to reach into a thousand people groups. We'll have to get better at connecting with new students online, not just maintaining real-life relationships. The future of all campus ministry may look like what's happening at community colleges around the country—large but disjointed student bodies, moving targets that are exceedingly difficult to reach.

3. Non-traditional students will become more traditional.

As online education expands and economic forces change people's plans, we'll have fewer "traditional" students (full-time students for four to five years who are eighteen to twenty-two) and more non-traditional students. We'll need to be prepared for a number of different kinds of students, including older students who have to balance their coursework with raising a family or students who to save money overload on their credit hours so they can graduate early. We may also work more often with part-time students or those who are only with us for a year or two after transferring from a community college.

In addition to non-traditional students, we'll also need to adapt our methodologies to appeal to students of differing ethnic and racial backgrounds and cultures. Many college settings remain overwhelmingly white, but as the demographics of North America continue to shift toward a majority of minorities, Higher Ed is following suit. These numbers include international students, but the majority are comprised of national African-Americans, Latinos, and Asians, with a staggering diversity *within* these groups.

We should also be ready for a shifting gender balance on campus. Just a couple generations ago, women were striving for equal access to campus. Now, the U.S. Department of Education projects that by 2019, women will account for 59 percent of total undergraduate enrollment and 61 percent of total postbaccalaureate enrollment at the nation's colleges and universities.[4] Of course, college ministry already sees more involvement from women than men. So should we expect an even higher level of gender imbalance? While the gains of women are certainly to be celebrated, the new gender gap is not without its consequences for the social environment of our campuses and ministries. Hard as it may be to believe, campus ministers may need to begin to take into account the unique needs and preferences of men (the minority) in how we approach ministry.

4. College ministers may face diminished access to secular campuses.

As societal norms continue to shift from traditional Christian ones, many ministries may find that they challenge university regulations and speech codes. A notable example is the Hastings case of 2010, in which the Supreme Court ruled that a university-sanctioned Christian student organization could not restrict membership to those who affirmed their beliefs.[5] In recent years, cases at Eastern Michigan, Illinois, Wisconsin, Ohio State, Rutgers, and other universities have raised similar issues. The *shibboleth* of homosexuality, in particular, could make it increasingly difficult for Christian student organizations to get funding, room reservations, and other accommodations. It could also effectively bar those of us who don't have reasons besides ministry from walking on campus.

It is likely that these sorts of cases will become increasingly common, and some organizations will elect to fight this battle legally. What will be our posture? While we certainly have some rights worth protecting, relying on the law alone is a losing strategy. Going through the courts will be incredibly costly in time, energy, money, and our witness to the campus. Eventually, many more campus ministries may have to figure out how to function without full university recognition or legal sanction.

We ought to be working on navigating the coming challenges with grace and humility, adding value and generally seeking to bless our campuses, and planning the future model of our ministry in the event that we have to go "underground." If we equip students to lead and disciple other students rather than depending on staff, our ministry, and more importantly, the spread of the gospel on campus, will be better able to absorb loss of access. We should also work hard at cultivating connections with those Christians who already have access—faculty and staff.

In an issue of *Christianity Today*, historian Mark Noll reminded readers that in the 1940s and '50s, it was commonly believed that evangelical Christians had "lost China" because the Communists had expelled missionaries.[6] In retrospect, that change was likely the best thing to happen to the Chinese church because native Chinese Christians were forced to lead and work toward creating uniquely Chinese expressions of their faith. Now, the Chinese church is perhaps the largest in the world. If we in college ministry lose access to our campuses, might we see a similar spiritual resurgence among college students?

5. Financial sustainability will be challenged.

For many of us, raising support is an integral part of our ministry; it is often both a joy and a frustration of our work. What will the future hold for this aspect of ministry? Support raising is predicated on a sizable base of potential donors with a predisposition toward giving to our ministries. Thousands of us have been able to head out to the campus mission field because of the generosity of our financial partners. But the next ten years will likely mark a significant decrease in the North American base of ministry funding, as approximately 100,000 churches will disappear. The World War II generation will be gone, and the Baby Boomers (now at the peak of their earning power) will transition from giving to organizations like ours to receiving Social Security, Medicare, and the like on reduced incomes. These changes could fundamentally reshape the landscape for support raising.

General giving patterns are also changing. With the advent of micro-lending, donors want not only access, but specificity and control. It seems that people are no longer content to let their gift be a drop in the bucket. They want to know exactly what it will be used for. So where does that leave us? The overall donor base will shrink, and competition for funding will increase.

One possible solution is to tap into other potential sources of income. The entire field of campus ministry may need to become more bivocational in nature, while simultaneously looking to those Christians already employed on our campuses—faculty and staff whom God has already burdened for lost students and who are uniquely positioned to reach them.

Looking to the Future

I can't say with certainty that any or all of these disruptions will happen or to what degree they will change college ministry. My concern is not so much these issues themselves but how we respond to them. Neither blithely ignoring them nor belatedly reacting to them will help us grow and thrive in the future. If we are instead proactive, trusting the God who has shepherded his church through challenges far worse than these, we will once again be proven faithful as we work to create fruitful college ministries and effective disciples—in whatever context we find ourselves ministering.

We don't know what will happen in the future, but we know who is in charge of it. While the Western world has passed from Christendom, Christianity will never pass from the world (see Matthew 16). Jesus isn't afraid of the future. And he wants us to try new things. In fact, he *loves* new things: "'I am making everything new!'" (Revelation 21:5). As we embrace the future and make something new for the kingdom, let us remember that our genuine innovation is really *renovation* and flows from Jesus' renewing kingdom work.

Chapter 15
MARCHING ORDERS

The disciples don't know what they don't know about Jesus, but that doesn't stop Jesus from sending them out.

In Matthew 10, Jesus gives his twelve disciples the first of several commissionings to go in his name, preaching the kingdom of heaven. This sending follows his words in Matthew 9:37-38: "'The harvest is plentiful but the workers are few. Ask the Lord of the harvest, therefore, to send out workers into his harvest field.'" Jesus' response to the need he sees is to impart that same vision of the plentiful harvest to his disciples and to send them out immediately to do something about it.

At this point in the narrative, the disciples don't know what will happen to them. They can't fully understand much of what Jesus has taught them. They aren't even sure who Jesus is! (Peter's confession that Jesus is the Christ doesn't occur until chapter 16, and even then he goes on to say something that earns him a stiff rebuke.) The disciples don't know what they don't know about Jesus, but that doesn't stop Jesus from sending them out. For forty-two verses in chapter 10, Matthew gives us Jesus' marching orders—clear, practical instructions for the mission on which they're about to embark.

While respecting the differences between the disciples' situation and our own, we can certainly see some parallels and our need for Jesus' instructions for our own mission. When we step on campus, we also head into a mission field with a lot of uncertainty about ourselves and our ministries. And, certainly, we will make mistakes. We will enter into intimidating situations. But despite all that, Jesus sends us anyway. Like the disciples, we need practical instructions so we can be faithful to the mission. With that in mind, here are some "What do I do now?" marching orders for your ministry to the campus.

1. Depend on Jesus, covering your ministry in prayer

In Matthew 9:37-38, Jesus talks to the disciples about the plentiful harvest and the need for more laborers. So before sending them out, he teaches them to pray. We also must learn to pray if our work is to produce fruit. While our prayers will certainly be for ourselves, we also need to pray for laborers with whom we can share the work. And when we pray for our students, we should pray not only for our ministry *to* them, but for our ministry *with* them so that in a very real way, they would join us in this work.

Prayer has a profound ability to reorient us to the reality that we desperately need Jesus. Without prayer, we often default to one of two mentalities: "I can do it myself!" (if we think things are going well) or "It's hopeless!" (if things are not). Prayer reminds us that "'apart from [Christ we] can do nothing'" (John 15:5). Jesus wants us to depend on him. He told the disciples not to bring their money or their possessions because he knew that more than anything else, they needed to bring a prayerful dependency. Even today, prayer is the prerequisite for fruitful ministry.

Action Steps:
- Spend some time reflecting on your prayer practices. (See the diagnostic questions that follow.)
- Prioritize prayer as part of your job description. Make it a growth goal for yourself and the ministry.
- Schedule regular prayer walks, prayer retreats, and prayer meetings, both alone and with other staff members and students.
- Read a book to jumpstart your prayers, such as *A Praying Life* by Paul Miller.[1]

Questions:
- Does my prayer life include my asking God to provide more co-laborers, or am I just expecting God to help me do all the work alone?
- How frequent is my prayer life? How living and vital is it?
- What is the *content* of my prayer life? Am I praying me-centered prayers or harvest-focused prayers?

2. Remember your calling

The first thing Jesus does in Matthew 10 is call his disciples over to be with him. Matthew then names them, underscoring that real, ordinary, imperfect humans are being sent out on this mission. When we're out in the harvest field, we have to remember our callings—that God has called us into salvation, called us by name, and called us his very own children. Regularly reminding ourselves of our identity in Christ as saved, beloved children will sustain us against doubts, fears, and attacks.

We must also remember our call to ministry. We each entered college ministry for several reasons. What were those reasons? Hopefully, you believe God has given you unique gifts, abilities, and experiences in order to serve students. What are they? Are you utilizing them and developing them? In all this, we remember it is because God has called us and because he promises to continue that work that we can do anything. Regularly reminding yourself of who you are in Christ, and how God has called you to this work, is an essential part of sustaining a faithful ministry.

Much of what Jesus says in Matthew 10 focuses on what the disciples should expect when they go out in his name: some will accept them and their message, but others will reject them. Some will receive, but others will oppose. Some will open their doors, but others will throw them in jail. Although the opposition may look different today, we will face rejection. Jesus tells his followers to expect it. It's at these moments that our sense of calling becomes extremely important. Being rejected isn't easy, which is why we must remember that we're right where God wants us doing the work he has called us to do.

Action Steps:

- Identify a spiritual discipline that encourages you in your calling. Build it into your regular daily, weekly, and monthly rhythms.
- Identify a person who excels at building you up and affirming your calling. Make plans to meet or talk with this person regularly.
- Read resources that help you understand your gospel calling, such as *The Gospel Centered Life* by Bob Thune and Will Walker[2] or *The Prodigal God* by Tim Keller,[3] and your ministry calling, such as *The Call* by Os Guinness[4] or *The Fabric of Faithfulness* by Steve Garber.[5]

Questions for Calling:

- Do I have a clear, unshakeable sense of God's saving work in my life? Do I know how to continually preach that to myself?
- Do I have a clear sense of my calling to minister to college students? Can I articulate that to myself and others?

- How do I handle rejection? Do I fight back? Do I run away? Do I know how to reaffirm my identity in Christ even when people reject me?
- Do the people in my ministry understand their callings? How am I helping them discover them?

3. Go with Christ's authority

Whenever Jesus commissions people, he gives them his authority. The best example of this is in The Great Commission, Matthew 28:18-19, when he says, "'All authority in heaven and on earth has been given to me. Therefore go and make disciples of all nations.'" We go because Jesus has *all* authority, and we go on the basis of his authority.

It is essential we remember this because the question of authority will be thrown at us again and again in a number of forms: "Who are you to think your religion is the only way?" "Who do you think you are to tell me what I'm doing is wrong?" "Why do you think your interpretation of the Bible is the right one?" We must make clear that our ministries do not originate from our opinions or experiences, but from Christ's authority, the one who is the author of everything, the one by whom all things were created and in whom all things are held together (see Colossians 1).

Our understanding that we are commissioned under Christ's authority has profound implications for how we view leadership. Authoritarian leaders are not living under Christ's authority. Instead, we recognize that we must submit to him. Going with Christ's authority means that we recognize we're under his authority, which should make us both humble and strong.

Action Steps:

- Study a new aspect of Christ's authority in creation, looking for his fingerprint (the image of God) in science, literature, government, technology or another area outside of your expertise.
- Ask people who know you well for some honest feedback. Are you humble? Are you confident? Do you combine these traits in a Christ-like way? Do you evidence someone who is living under Christ's authority?

Questions for Authority:

- Do I ground my ministry in the authority of Jesus Christ? Does my confidence come from being right or from being made righteous in Christ?
- Do I display the humility of one who is under the authority of Christ?
- When disagreements arise, do I distinguish between biblical principles and my (or others') opinions?

4. To whom are you going?

At this stage of Jesus' ministry in Matthew 10, he wanted the disciples to preach to the Jews only, not the Gentiles or Samaritans (verse 5), though eventually he and the apostles did reach those groups. Part of Jesus' reasoning—among some other big picture theological reasons—was the simple practicality of reining in and focusing their task. They couldn't reach everybody at once, and Jesus probably knew that if they didn't focus their evangelism, they would quickly become overwhelmed and give up.

In the same way, your campus is made up of hundreds of people groups. You can't reach them all—at least not at first. So to whom should you reach out? With which particular segments of the campus population should you seek to connect, asking, "How do I communicate the timeless truth of the gospel, the message of the kingdom of God, to these ever-changing groups of people?" No matter which groups on which you choose to focus your time and attention, communicating the gospel will come through our words and our actions, telling them in ways they understand that "the kingdom of heaven is near," and being agents of healing, redemption, reconciliation, and new life.

Action Steps:

- Spend time on your school's website. Find out how many student organizations there are. Start creating a short list of the groups with whom you'd like to connect.
- Spend significant time in conversation with students from the groups on your short list. Ask questions, but let them do most of the talking. Discover what they love, what they hate, what they celebrate,

what they fear, what they have in common, what they disagree on, and anything else that distinguishes them.

- Pray for a "person of peace," someone who can open doors for you and give you access to a group that would normally not allow you time with them or proximity to them.
- Start developing a ministry strategy that takes into account what makes these groups unique.

Questions for Target Groups:

- How has God made me? What are my experiences, and how do they overlap with student groups? Where's my greatest interest?
- Which groups are being overlooked or neglected? To which of these groups could I reach out? Where's the greatest need?
- For whom does my heart break?

Let me close this book with a prayer for these things:

Father,

I thank you for the gospel transformation that you have worked in my life. I thank you that you have called me to the ministry of gospel transformation among college students and in higher education. I thank you for your grace, by which all this is possible.

For the sake of your glory and the spread of your kingdom, I commit myself to regularly praying for my campus and my students. I will seek to cultivate my calling and theirs according to your will, grounding it in the gospel. I will seek to keep your mission front and center, and not revert to internally-focused ministry. I will seek to grow in wisdom in how to reach my campus. Please give me wisdom, humility, grace, patience, and a heart that breaks like yours for those who are far from you. Let me not stop at gathering a crowd, but let me make disciples who will go out on mission.

I commit to seeking and building unity with other churches and ministries that also love you. Keep me from being jealous, uncharitable, or ungenerous. In all things, at all times, let me be faithful to you, your mission, and your call on my life, so that my students and my campus may be transformed.

In Jesus' name,

Amen

Now get out there and change your campus to change the world!

NOTES

Introduction

1. "Campus Philly: The Students' Insider Guide to Philly," Issuu, accessed January 23, 2011, http://issuu.com/campusphilly/docs/studentguide2010.

Chapter One

1. Tom Clegg and Warren Bird, *Lost in America: How You and Your Church Can Impact the World Next Door,* Loveland, CO: Group Publishing, 2001, 25.

2. Christian Smith, "Getting a Life: The Challenge of Emerging Adulthood," *Books & Culture,* November/December 2007.

3. Kelly Monroe Kullberg, *Finding God Beyond Harvard: The Quest for Veritas,* Downers Grove, IL: InterVarsity Press, 2006, 84.

4. T. S. Eliot, "The Waste Land," 1922, in *The Waste Land and Other Writings,* New York: Random House, 2002, 38-57.

5. Mark J. Penn, *Microtrends: The Small Forces Behind Tomorrow's Big Changes,* New York: Hachette Book Group, 2007.

6. For an excellent example of Powlison's Three Trees model at work, read Nina Campagna's "Yelling at My Kids" at http://www.ccef.org/yelling-my-kids, August 2, 2010.

7. Jonathan Dodson, "Missional Communities in Cities and Suburbs," accessed February 1, 2011, http://www.jonathandodson.org/wp-content/uploads/2009/09/missional-communities-in-cities-and-suburbs.pdf.

8. Some of the above information on trees taken from "10 Amazing and Magnificent Trees in the World," The Best Article Every Day, accessed February 3, 2011, http://www.bspcn.com/2007/12/15/10-amazing-and-magnificent-trees-in-the-world/.

Chapter Two

1. "Tim Keller: Biographical Sketch," Monergism.com, accessed March 5, 2011, http://www.monergism.com/thethreshold/articles/bio/timkeller.html.

2. David T. Olson, *The American Church in Crisis: Groundbreaking Research Based on a National Database of over 200,000 Churches,* Grand Rapids: Zondervan, 2008.

3. http://www.census.gov/PressRelease/www/releases/archives/facts_for_features_special_editions/002263.html, accessed March 11, 2011.

4. "State of Campus Ministry 2008," The Ivy Jungle, accessed March 11, 2011, http://www.ivyjungle.org/state-of-campus-ministry-2-8.

5. Michael Green, *Sharing Your Faith with Friends and Family: Talking about Jesus Without Offending,* Grand Rapids: Baker, 2005, 27.

6. Steve Lutz, "Resources: Ivy Jungle State of Campus Ministry 2006," The SEN-Tinel: Thoughts on Gospel, Mission, Culture, Innovation, & Campus Ministry, http://stevelutz.files.wordpress.com/state-of-campus-ministry-2006.ppt, no longer available as of July 1, 2011.

7. Thom S. Rainer, "Five Major Trends for Churches in America," May 10, 2010, http://www.thomrainer.com/2010/05/five-major-trends-for-churches-in-america.php.

8. David Kinnaman and Gabe Lyons, UnChristian: What a New Generation Really Thinks about Christianity . . . And Why It Matters, Grand Rapids: Baker, 2007, 25.

9. Ed Stetzer, Richie Stanley, and Jason Hayes, Lost and Found: The Younger Unchurched and the Churches that Reach Them, Nashville: B&H, 2009, 32, 60.

10. Milton J. Coalter, John M. Mulder, and Louis B. Weeks, The Re-Forming Tradition: Presbyterians and Mainstream Protestantism, Louisville, KY: Westminster/John Knox, 1992, 258.

Chapter Three

1. Dan Kimball, The Emerging Church: Vintage Christianity for New Generations, Grand Rapids: Zondervan/Youth Specialties, 2003, 94.

2. Tim Keller, "The Missional Church," June 2001, www.redeemer2.com/resources/papers/missional.pdf. Theologian Lesslie Newbigin makes a helpful distinction worth noting here, between the church's missionary dimension and its missionary intention: the church is both "missionary" and "missionizing." Also, see David J. Bosch's summary section entitled, "Missionary by its very nature," in Transforming Mission, Maryknoll, NY: Orbis, 1991, 372-73. Keller is speaking of the church's missionizing efforts, which flow from its missionary nature, a nature itself based on God's own missionary nature.

3. Tim Keller, "The Missional Church," June 2001, www.redeemer2.com/resources/papers/missional.pdf.

Chapter Four

1. Quoted in John G. Flett, The Witness of God: The Trinity, Missio Dei, Karl Barth, and the Nature of Christian Community, Grand Rapids: Eerdmans, 2010, 71.

2. C. S. Lewis, The Joyful Christian, New York: Touchstone, 1996, 138. First published 1977 by Macmillan.

Chapter Five

1. "Engaging the University," Prof. John Stackhouse's Weblog, accessed March 24, 2011, http://stackblog.wordpress.com/engaging-the-university/.

2. Jeffrey Jensen Arnett, Emerging Adulthood: The Winding Road from the Late Teens through the Twenties, New York: Oxford UP, 2004. This book redefined the study of the transitions people make through their teens and twenties.

Chapter Six

1. Alan Hirsch, The Forgotten Ways: Reactivating the Missional Church, Grand Rapids: Brazos, 2006. Hirsch's books have had a profound effect on missional ministry around the world as well as the ministry described here.

2. Tim Keller, "Ministry in the New Global Culture of Major City-Centers: Part I," The Gospel Coalition, http://www.thegospelcoalition.org/resources/a/Ministry-in-the -New-Global-Culture-of-Major-City-Centers-Part-I, no longer available as of July 1, 2011.

3. Christian Smith and Patricia Snell, *Souls in Transition: The Religious and Spiritual Lives of Emerging Adults,* New York: Oxford UP, 2009.

4. "Religion Among the Millennials," The Pew Forum on Religion & Public Life, February 17, 2010, http://pewforum.org/Age/Religion-Among-the-Millennials.aspx#beliefs.

5. Alan Hirsch, *The Forgotten Ways: Reactivating the Missional Church,* Grand Rapids: Brazos, 2006, 127-48.

Chapter Eight

1. Dietrich Bonhoeffer, *The Cost of Discipleship,* New York: Touchstone, 1995, 59. Translated from the German Nachfolge first published 1937 by Chr. Kaiser Verlag Munchen by R. H. Fuller.

2. The following is an excellent case study on missional ministry at University of Texas-Austin: Amy Ferrara, "The Ascent of a Multi-Generational Missional Ministry at HCBC's University of Texas Church Plant," 2009, http://www.apollosleadership.org/ wp-content/uploads/2010/09/HCBC-UT-Case-Study_20091.pdf.

3. Eddie Gibbs and Ryan K. Bolger, *Emerging Churches: Creating Christian Community in Postmodern Cultures,* Grand Rapids: Baker Academic, 2005, 56.

4. Robert Webber, *Ancient-Future Evangelism: Making Your Church a Faith-Forming Community,* Grand Rapids: Baker, 2003, 42.

5. Dietrich Bonhoeffer, *The Cost of Discipleship,* New York: Touchstone, 1995, 89. Translated from the German Nachfolge first published 1937 by Chr. Kaiser Verlag Munchen by R. H. Fuller.

6. Robert Webber, *Ancient-Future Evangelism: Making Your Church a Faith-Forming Community,* Grand Rapids: Baker, 2003, 44-46.

7. Ibid, 71.

8. I'm borrowing this phrase from Tim Keller.

9. Jeffrey Arnold, *Small Group Outreach: Turning Groups Inside Out,* Downers Grove, IL: InterVarsity, 1998, 23.

Chapter Nine

1. David Bosch, *Mission and Evangelism,* Calcutta: ISPCK, 1998, 21.

2. Robert E. Coleman, *The Master Plan of Evangelism,* Second Edition, Abridged, Grand Rapids: Spire, 2006, 27.

Chapter Ten

1. "Penn Gillette [Jillette] Gets a Gift of a Bible," YouTube, August 4, 2009, http:// www.youtube.com/watch?v=ZhG-tkQ_Q2w.

2. Joe Paosnanski, "Joe Paterno Top of the World, Pa!" *Sports Illustrated,* October 26, 2009, http://sportsillustrated.cnn.com/vault/article/magazine/MAG1161606/3/ index.htm.

3. Mark Oestreicher, *Youth Ministry 3.0: A Manifesto of Where We've Been, Where We Are & Where We Need to Go,* Grand Rapids: Zondervan, 2008, 108.

4. Seth Godin, *Linchpin: Are You Indispensable?* New York: Portfolio, 2010, 118-19.

Chapter Twelve

1. See various confessions from the Reformation period, including The Confession of the English Congregation at Geneva (1556), the French Confession of Faith (1559), articles 26-28; the Scottish Confession of Faith (1560), chapters 16 and 18, and the Belgic Confession of Faith (1561), articles 27-29; Second Helvetic Confession (1566), chapter 17.

2. Neil Cole, *Organic Leadership: Leading Naturally Right Where You Are,* Grand Rapids, MI: Baker, 2009, 116.

Chapter Thirteen

1. Charles Habib Malik, *A Christian Critique of the University,* Downers Grove, IL: InterVarsity, 1982, 100-01.

2. Paul Dwight Moody and Arthur Percy Fitt, *The Shorter Life of D. L. Moody,* Chicago: The Bible Institute, 1900, 79.

3. Two highly regarded lists are produced by Shanghai Jiao Tong University at http://www.arwu.org/index.jsp and by QS at http://www.topuniversities.com/university-rankings/world-university-rankings/2010.

4. Kevin O'Connor, "International Students and Global Cities," *GaWC Research Bulletin,* February 17, 2005, http://www.lboro.ac.uk/gawc/rb/rb161.html.

5. Karin Fischer, "Number of Foreign Students in U.S. Hit a New High Last Year," *The Chronicle of Higher Education,* November 16, 2009, http://chronicle.com/article/Number-of-Foreign-Students-/49142/.

6. Charles Habib Malik, *A Christian Critique of the University,* Downers Grove, IL: InterVarsity, 1982, 100-01.

Chapter Fourteen

1. Henry Ford, *My Life and Work,* Fairfield, Iowa: Akasha Classics, 2008. First published 1922.

2. "11 of the Dumbest Business Decisions Ever," The Best Article Every Day, March 20, 2010, http://www.bspcn.com/2008/04/22/11-of-the-dumbest-business-decisions-ever/.

3. Quoted in Calvin Miller, *Preaching: The Art of Narrative Exposition,* Grand Rapids: Baker, 2006, 241.

4. Peter Schmidt, "Men's Share of College Enrollments Will Continue to Dwindle, Federal Report Says," *The Chronicle of Higher Education,* May 27, 2010, http://chronicle.com/article/Mens-Share-of-College/65693/.

5. Cathy Young, "Hastings Case Sets a Dangerous Precedent," *Real Clear Politics,* July 1, 2010, http://www.realclearpolitics.com/articles/2010/07/01/hastings_case_sets_a_dangerous_precedent_106164.html.

6. Mark Noll, interview by David Neff, "Does Global Christianity Equal American Christianity?" *Christianity Today,* July 8, 2009, http://www.christianitytoday.com/ct/2009/july/19.38.html.

Chapter Fifteen

1. Paul E. Miller, *A Praying Life: Connecting with God in a Distracting World,* Colorado Springs: NavPress, 2009.

2. Bob Thune and Will Walker, *The Gospel Centered Life,* Greensboro, NC: New Growth Press, 2011.

3. Tim Keller, *The Prodigal God,* New York: Penguin, 2008.

4. Os Guinness, *The Call,* Nashville, TN: Thomas Nelson, 2003.

5. Steve Garber, *The Fabric of Faithfulness,* Downers Grove, IL: InterVarsity, 1996.